MAKING FOOD THAT IS BOTH HEALTHFUL AND DELICIOUS— and easy on the planet—is way easier than you might think. It's about relinquishing the stress of making the "right" choices and just focusing on making better ones. It's being conscious of—but not obsessed with—how we eat. It's knowing that converting to veganism is fine, but realistically, big change is possible if we all just discover how good a bowl of beans with a little smoked pork can be.

With more than ninety recipes for simple yet stunning food, and thoughtful tips on how to hack your kitchen, home, and life, Sam explains how the food system really works, and how easy, small, tasty choices add up to enormous change.

EAT a little BETTER

EAT a little BETTER

Great Flavor, Good Health, Better World

SAM KASS

CLARKSON POTTER/PUBLISHERS
NEW YORK

for CY MINDON KASS

CONTENTS

1 / INTRODUCTION

INTRODUCTION

WHO I AM, AND HOW WE CAN CHANGE OUR HEALTH AND HELP THE WORLD

The Secret Service *hates* it when you run in the White House. Sudden movement isn't exactly their thing. But the agents stationed inside 1600 Pennsylvania Avenue soon got used to the sight of me sprinting down the corridors, past portraits of ex-presidents and toward the kitchen.

I can't count the times that I was absorbed in some important meeting and glanced at my watch, only to realize it was almost 6 p.m., and I had just half an hour to get dinner on the table for a family of four, including a man who didn't exactly have time to wait. Despite his busy schedule, President Obama almost always made it back to the Residence by 6:30 to eat with Michelle and their two girls. It was an inspiring sight—the busiest man in the world carving out time for this daily ritual. I'd excuse myself from the meeting and just start booking it through the West Wing.

At the White House, I had two jobs: to work on food and nutrition policy and to cook dinner for the president and his family. I spent an hour or so a day making nutritious, delicious food for the First Family, but worked most of my waking hours to help families around the country do the same in their homes.

A job at the White House comes with no blueprint. The learning curve is steep for anyone, and especially for a guy who hadn't spent a day in politics. Before I came to the White House, I was a cook moonlighting as a food-policy geek. But I quickly became a food-policy guy who knew how to cook. I traded chef whites for suits and sweaty restaurant kitchens for the conference rooms in the Eisenhower Executive Office Building (or the EEOB, one of the thousands of mind-numbing acronyms you learn when working in government). Instead of searing fish against hot iron, I was steering meetings with the First Lady, senior staffers, public health experts, and economists. And with the First Lady leading the charge, we launched the biggest public health campaign to come out of the White House in American history.

But this book isn't the story of that campaign—not exactly. It's about the lessons I learned fighting for change in D.C. that can change the way you eat at home. It's about learning the little choices that add up to make you happier and the planet healthier—and your dinners more delicious—without stressing about the big, life-changing choices that just aren't realistic. It's about how to stop worrying about eating "right" and just start eating a little better.

★

A DECADE BEFORE I FELL INTO POLITICS, I was a college kid who fell in love with the culture of the restaurant kitchen.

Then a screwed-up sauce sent me down a new path.

I was twenty when I left junior college, where I'd been playing baseball and hoping to get drafted into the majors. Once I realized I was good but not good enough, I enrolled at the University of Chicago and studied history. I spent my final semester in Vienna. I didn't care where I went. I just wanted to see the world.

When I arrived, I told the director of the program that I was interested in food and cooking. (Vienna, after all, is the pastry capital of the world.) In one of many ridiculous bits of good luck that got me where I am today, the director had a connection—I kid you not, her husband's uncle's friend from college had a son who rode bicycles with the sous chef at Moerwald, one of the best restaurants in the city.

She arranged for me to meet the sous chef, so the next afternoon, I found myself navigating the narrow streets in the old part of the city until I reached the corner where we were supposed to meet. Across the street, I saw a man pushing a fancy racing bike. He was decked out in cycling spandex, a black bandanna, and large Prada sunglasses. His arms were covered with homemade brandings. He looked like the kind of guy you should slowly back away from. Both of us stood there, waiting, for five minutes, until to my surprise he started walking across the street in my direction. I looked away as he got closer. I didn't want him to catch me staring. When I looked up again, I was face to face with those sunglasses. "So," he said. "You're the Yankee who wants to cook."

I was a college kid who fell in love with the culture of the restaurant kitchen.

This was Alois Traint, my new boss and soon-to-be mentor. From day one, I was in awe of Alois. As the sous chef at the Michelin-starred Moerwald, he cut a different figure than he did on the street. He traded his wacky gear for a spotless white chef's coat and an array of razor-sharp, wildly expensive knives. He called out orders from his spotless station, oversaw the cooks, and plated every single dish with dozens of sauces and garnishes, all fastidiously labeled. He was a machine and, to this day, the best cook I've ever worked with.

My plan was to cook occasionally and study often. What actually happened was the opposite. By the end of my first shift, a brutal but invigorating ten-hour tryout, I was hooked. Everyone in the small kitchen—just four cooks and Alois—worked with a controlled ferocity at a breakneck pace but with striking skill. While on the other side of the doors the dining room hummed quietly, the kitchen was alive with clanking pans, whirring blenders, hissing fat, and the rat-a-tat of knives reducing vegetables to tiny, perfect pieces. It was thunderous, but not noise. The sound had order to it, like an orchestra playing a strange, exhilarating piece of music. And Alois was the conductor. His players presented him with the elements of each dish and he united them on the plate with a workman's skill and an artist's eye.

At the end of dinner service, Alois called me over to meet Christian Domschitz, the restaurant's head chef. Christian handed me a fat, raw scallop on a half-inch-wide spatula and told me to bring this to a cook on the other side of the kitchen. I was confused—he didn't have a plate to put the scallop on?—but with the kitchen staff all watching me, I made like I was playing center field again, shutting out the distractions that turned a simple task into a difficult one. Scallop safely delivered, Christian said, "You're welcome back in my kitchen any time." (Only a year later did he explain that it was a test: You can teach a cook to make anything, he said, but you can't teach a steady hand.)

After just a few days in the kitchen, school became my last concern. I came to love cooking for many of the same reasons I had loved baseball—the nonstop learning, the challenge of performing every day, and the particular kind of pressure. Unlike basketball and football, baseball is both a team sport and an individual one. Cooking, too, is a group struggle where an individual can ruin everything with one mistake. And in the beginning, I made many.

One night early on in my time there, I was working as *garde manger*, the lowest rung of the kitchen stations. For the most part, I made salads. Occasionally I made a simple component of an elaborate cooked dish. That night, a table of ten people had ordered—for the kitchen, that kicked off the task of preparing all ten dishes so they'd be ready at the same time. The task was complicated, but not difficult, at least not for cooks as skilled as those at Moerwald. Seeing them reminded me of watching a top infield turn a double play—it appears effortless only because the players are so damn good at it. I wanted to be that good at cooking.

With just a few words quietly spoken, the cooks deftly coordinated their searing, sautéing, and roasting, even as Alois called out orders from other tables. Soon Alois had all ten dishes in front of him, nearly ready to be served. Just one of those dishes was missing something. "Yankee!" he yelled. "I need the crostini." And of course, even though all I had to do was fry bread in butter and slather on saffron aïoli, I'd forgotten the crostini. Rather than sacrifice perfection by letting the food languish for the five minutes it would've taken me to fix my mistake, Alois dumped it all in the trash. All that work had been for nothing, and every cook in that kitchen knew who was to blame. Fortunately, baseball also prepares you to handle failure well; it's a sport in which failing to get a hit seven out of ten times earns you a .300 batting average and a pretty good shot at the Hall of Fame.

I learned from these mistakes. (I certainly never forgot another crostini.) In fact, learning was the primary currency I accepted in exchange for my labor.

ALOIS TRAINT, MY FORMER BOSS AND MENTOR

Alois and Christian also fed me breakfast, lunch, and dinner and sometimes slipped me pocket money. Alois even started staying at his girlfriend's place so I could crash at his apartment and not have to pay rent. Almost every day, I woke up, met Christian for breakfast, prepped and cooked lunch, raced to class, and returned to the restaurant to prep and cook dinner. Afterwards, I went out with Alois and Christian, who were treated like culinary royalty wherever they went. I was a broke, rookie cook who spent his off-hours drinking fancy Austrian white wines and smoking cigars. I like to think they admired my hustle, but I suspect they also got a kick out of the American kid who chose to cube carrots all day.

When I graduated from college, I came right back to Vienna and Moerwald, lack of work permit be damned. I even got promoted, albeit inadvertently. The saucier had just left to have surgery, and Christian had to fill in. He was not happy about it. As head chef, he had toiled for many years to break free from kitchen drudgery, yet now here he was, back to chopping vegetables, making stocks, and filleting fish. So he enlisted me, the kitchen's lowliest cook, to do his grunt work. Suddenly, I had a highly motivated mentor giving me a crash course in one of the kitchen's top jobs. The faster I learned, the less work he had to do. In a matter of weeks, I learned how to prepare every meat, fish, and sauce they served. That's when my perspective changed forever.

ONE DAY, WE WERE PREPPING FOR DINNER SERVICE. Alois had told me to make the rhubarb sauce for a dish of seared foie gras. His initial instructions, delivered in his thick Viennese accent, were to cook the rhubarb, then mix in plenty of butter—and let's just say he used much more colorful language than that. But I didn't know how much butter he meant. So after cooking the rhubarb, I put a fist-sized knob of it into the saucepan. As I whisked, he stared at me with his piercing eyes and a look of such contempt that you'd think I'd just poured the sauce onto the floor. "Yankee," he said.

He repeated his command, and eager to please him, I added another giant chunk, but no dice. He moved me aside and deposited a slab of butter so large that my heart hurt just looking at it. He whisked furiously as he dressed me down. "It's not my problem if customers walk out of here and drop dead of a heart attack!" he said. "They ask us to make food that tastes good, not food that's good for them." And you know what? He was right.

"It's not my problem if customers walk out of here and drop dead!" he said.

Still, that moment rocked me. Not because I had let Alois down, but because I suddenly saw the disturbing truth in what he said. We were cooking without regard for the consequences of what we served, and people were eating without regard for the consequences of what they ate.

People's personal indulgences are all well and good, but what I couldn't get behind was that I *shouldn't care* about these consequences. And so I began to wonder: What exactly were those consequences? As I got back to work, distracted by this question, I saw the kitchen's back door swing open and watched one of our purveyors enter, pushing a hand truck stacked with birds—five crates of chickens, ducks, and eggs. Now my mind was really churning. If what I put on the plate had consequences for the people eating it, surely it also had consequences for the people who raised the animals and farmed the vegetables, and for the land they used. Once I had asked myself these questions, there was no going back.

In my spare time, I put down cookbooks and picked up books about the American food system (shipped to me by my patient mother), entering a wonkish world of anthropology and history, science and policy. It quickly became apparent that the consequences of our diet were more serious than I had ever imagined.

I gaped at statistics on the surging rates of obesity, diabetes, and heart disease in the United States, rereading them and thinking they couldn't possibly be right. I learned that slabs of goose liver and buttery sauces, however, were not the heart of the problem. Those chilling stats were clearly linked not to the rarefied world of fine dining, but to the modern transformation of how we produce the vast majority of our food. I pored over tomes on the history of agriculture, tracing the creeping dominion of massive farms growing primarily three crops—wheat, soy, and corn—which in turn fueled a mammoth processed-food industry.

Along with the effects on our health, the environmental repercussions came into focus. Yet only years later would I come to understand that our food system's reliance on synthetic fertilizers, its lack of crop diversity, and its prolific meat production took a toll beyond polluted rivers and damaged soil. They were also contributing to a perilous change in the climate.

Back then, the notion of climate change had just started to enter the mainstream. When I began my research, I thought the culprit was fossil fuels, not food—belching smokestacks and highways clogged with cars, not belching cows and vast fields clogged with corn. Yet I learned that while energy is still the leading driver of greenhouse gas emissions, the production of food is a close second. Today, it accounts for somewhere between 25 and 30 percent of global greenhouse gas emissions. The direct impact seemed abstract—invisible gases causing a slight increase in global temperatures—but the consequences did not. A global increase of only a few degrees wouldn't just melt glaciers and raise sea levels, flooding countless low-lying cities around the world, but would also threaten the global food supply. The way we eat today, I realized, can play an important role in whether or not future generations will have enough to eat.

Suddenly, in a blur of books, bones, and butter, a year had passed since I had returned to work illegally in Vienna. Christian and Alois were as eager to keep me on as I was eager to stay—Alois even suggested that I marry his girlfriend—so they went to the restaurant's owner for help getting me the necessary work papers. The owner waved away our concerns—he was close friends, he claimed, with Austria's minister of the interior. Email him, he told me, and everything will be taken care of. So I did, not realizing that this was the equivalent of emailing the vice president of the United States and expecting him to help me secure a worker's permit as an illegal line cook. Surprisingly, the minister actually *did* read my email . . . which he immediately forwarded to the authorities. Soon I got word that if I didn't leave the country within a few days, they would make sure to provide an escort.

Everywhere I went, I saw food as the deepest expression of people's identities.

★

WOMAN IN TLAXCALA, MEXICO, MAKING TAMALES

ALTHOUGH I WAS SAD TO LEAVE, I WAS HAPPY TO HAVE the time to step up my research. For the next five years, I traveled on the cheap, turning my adventures into a sort of independent study of some of the world's great food cultures.

I became friends with a winemaker in Italy and joined him and his family for the harvest, hauling grapes, learning their process, and taking part in the family's annual slaughter of a pig, whose every part became food. I ate my way through Southeast Asia, watching street vendors stir-fry with the same rapt attention I'd devoted to watching Alois sauté. I traversed Peru, then canoed deep into the Amazon rain forest. I spent a week with a local guide who lived off the forest and knew every edible bark and vine; one pitch-black night he showed me how to kill, gut, and cook a caiman, cousin of the alligator.

I journeyed through Mexico to explore corn, one of the world's most important crops, in its birthplace. I shadowed a seed dealer in the north, where industrial agriculture reigned. I planted ancient varieties of corn with small farmers in Chiapas, who I only later found out were Zapatista rebels. For the Day of the Dead holiday, I joined grandmothers in Tlaxcala to help them make and hand out thousands of tamales—considered gifts from those who had passed on—by folding banana leaves around masa, dough made from field corn that's been soaked in alkaline water and then ground.

Everywhere I went, I saw food as the deepest expression of people's identities. In the Piedmont region of Italy, I watched a husband and wife who had grown up in neighboring towns argue with passion over the proper way to seal ravioli. ("You press it!" he said, endorsing his town's method. "No, you pinch it, you idiot!" she said, championing hers.) In Mexico, I learned corn was so vital to Mayans that it entered their religious origin story, in which gods ground it into masa and molded the first humans out of it. Alongside meals made with masa, a sort of preindustrial processed food that some say enabled the cultural sophistication of Mesoamerican peoples, I also saw the complicated meaning of modern food. In rural Mexico, the presence of bottles of Coke on the table, proudly placed there by my hosts, was a sign of newfound prosperity . . . and possibly a symbol of the coming obesity epidemic. In Rio de Janeiro, a friend's father—a legendary Brazilian jazz musician we called Leo the Lion—took me around, introducing me as a great chef, even though I was just a young cook. People responded with such reverence that it made me think about pursuing cooking as a career in a way I hadn't before. I wanted to do something that inspired such respect.

I put into practice some of the abstract notions I'd been reading about. My approach to health was to keep things simple.

★

WHEN I RAN OUT OF MONEY, I WENT BACK TO MY hometown of Chicago and scored a job as a line cook at Paul Kahan's incredible restaurant Avec, helmed at the time by chef Koren Grieveson. She schooled me in a new style of cooking. Instead of the elaborate, laborious dishes Alois and Christian favored, her food was unfussy and bold, with big flavors and great ingredients.

Then, about a year into my tenure, Carroll Joynes and Abby O'Neil, parents of a good friend, came in to the restaurant for dinner and we got to talking. They were building a vacation home in New Zealand and asked if I'd be willing to come cook for them for a few months. While I loved working at Avec, I hesitated for approximately one second before accepting the job. Soon I was living near Queenstown, and for the first time, no one was telling me what to cook.

Adventurous and thoughtful eaters, Carroll and Abby gave me only one instruction: Make simple, healthy food. At the time, this struck me as unusual and auspicious. Most people still subscribed to Alois's theory of eating—that flavor trumps all else. But I lucked out with a family whose desires coincided with my developing passion. They helped solidify my identity.

This was when I first put into practice some of the abstract notions I'd been reading about. To be successful, I knew I had to keep things simple. I'd ignore the conflicting science around which nutrients did what, and just buy vegetables, fruits, whole grains, and lean but tasty proteins. I'd focus on making them as delicious as I could, using some of the tricks I'd learned at restaurants. Sure, cooking in professional kitchens showed me the pleasures of potatoes mixed with their weight in butter, but it had also taught me the other elements of deliciousness—building flavor through basic cooking techniques, varying textures, and seasoning with acid and salt. Soon I was hooked on the challenge of cooking delicious food without resorting to butter and cream. My dream was to someday get involved in food politics and make major change, but for now, I was happy helping one family make progress.

After two New Zealand summers (bonus: skipping two Windy City winters), I moved back to chilly Chicago to pursue that dream of working in food politics and organizing chefs. I just didn't know how. Fortunately, luck intervened yet again.

THE WEEK I ARRIVED, CARROLL AND ABBY JUST happened to bump into an acquaintance of theirs who needed some help in the kitchen—a woman named Michelle Obama. It was the spring of 2007. Barack had announced his candidacy a few months earlier and was often on the road. Michelle was getting pulled into the campaign, while caring for Malia and Sasha and holding down a demanding job. The family's diet was suffering. Michelle wanted to make sure her kids ate good, healthy food.

Carroll and Abby just happened to bump into an acquaintance of theirs who needed some help in the kitchen—a woman named Michelle Obama.

I knew her from the small village-like world of Hyde Park, the neighborhood where Barack had taught at the University of Chicago. So Carroll and Abby put us in touch. Michelle and I agreed on a tryout.

Barack was on the road, so my audition would be cooking for Michelle and the girls. My culinary strategy was to let the market determine the menu. Peas had come into season. I bought a pound and then the chef part of my brain kicked in. I'd make fresh fettucine (kids like pasta, right?) with a vibrant, velvety sauce made from those sweet peas, some basil, a little lemon zest, and Parmesan. I made this meal in the Obamas' modest kitchen, rolling out pasta dough, seasoning and reseasoning the sauce until it was perfect. I plated it prettily and brought it to their dining room table, sure that I had killed my audition.

Well, it turns out that kids like spaghetti-and-meatballs pasta, not fancy pea-sauce pasta. Malia and Sasha were polite, but they clearly weren't feeling it. I spent that night bracing for rejection, replaying my decision over and over.

Fortunately, Michelle liked it, and after a few more meals, she told me she was eager to hire me. Barack, on the other hand, was not. Before he was a senator, he was a community organizer and a professor. At the time, he was a successful author, too, but he still balked at the idea of a private chef, even if I'd be cooking for them only three or four times a week. It just wasn't who he was. Michelle was frank with me about his reservations, but said she'd take care of it. And a few days later, she called me with an answer. "I told Barack he had two choices," she said. Either she would hire me to make sure the girls were getting good, healthy food and she would campaign for him, or she would do the cooking instead of campaigning. "Well," I asked, "what did he say?" And she replied, "He didn't say a thing."

While Barack and Michelle campaigned, her mother, Marian, held down the household and I held down the kitchen. A few weeks in, at Michelle's request, I gave their pantry a makeover, enlisting Sasha and Malia to help. To make it easier to eat well, we replaced the junk and put the real food front and center. (You can see the methods we used to do this on page 21.) In the kitchen, I quickly got to know my audience. In other words, I didn't cook any more pea-sauce pasta. Instead I channeled the same principles I had followed with Carroll and Abby. While what I cooked certainly represented change, the food wasn't puritanical, or even unfamiliar. There wasn't a sudden influx of spelt and flaxseeds, but I made

Every Day!
GREENS
EA
Every Day!

brown rice instead of white and I scaled back on the beef and pasta. There was still the occasional burger and bowl of spaghetti. The girls embraced it. Sasha especially loved to help me cook and became my little sous chef, pulling a chair up to the stove so she could watch and stir. I'd let her taste whatever I was making and ask her what it needed. "More lemon!" she'd say. "More salt!" And she was always right.

It didn't take long before Michelle understood the impact of these small changes. Not only did she feel great herself, but she also felt great about the health of her girls. Right around the time I started working for the Obamas, Michelle had taken the girls to their pediatrician. He had expressed concern over their test results. Those numbers, like those of so many kids he saw, were headed in a worrying direction. Over time, he told them, this could spell trouble. But when they returned, just a few months later, the doctor couldn't believe how quickly those numbers had improved.

They were eager to see what the fancy chef would come up with, and they were about to be thoroughly disappointed.

Moved by the dramatic results that had come from such simple changes, we began to discuss the challenges American families faced when they tried to feed their kids good food and how we could help. At her kitchen table, we would talk for hours. We dreamed of planting a garden on the South Lawn to make a statement about the importance of fresh, healthy food. We brainstormed how to make it easier for families to eat that food. We envisioned a national campaign to improve the health of kids. And then we laughed at ourselves, because at the time Barack was down thirty points in the polls, and winning seemed like the longest of long shots.

★

ON JANUARY 19, 2009, I WENT TO SLEEP AS THE GUY who makes dinner for the Obamas. The next morning, I woke up as the chef to the First Family. Turns out cooking for the First Family is a lot like cooking for any family, just with some unusual challenges. I learned this on my first day.

I scored a seat at the inauguration, tearing up as I took in the 1.8 million people who lined Pennsylvania Avenue and watched Justice John Roberts swear in our first African-American president. Then I raced to the White House to prepare dinner. This trip, just two miles from the Capitol, was complicated by perhaps the largest crowd ever to descend on Washington, D.C., and a security presence like you wouldn't believe.

When I finally got to the White House, only my second time there, I had barely any time to cook. It was a chaotic scene. That day, the Bushes were moving out, the Obamas were moving in, and couches, tables, and sprinting aides were everywhere. And then I showed up, the new guy, asking where the fridge was.

I was led to the small kitchen on the second floor of the the Residence. On the way, I met some of the ushers, butlers, cooks, and other members of the approximately hundred-person residential staff, some of whom had worked at the White House for thirty, forty, even fifty years. I was a strange sight—a nontraditional addition to the longtime kitchen team and a friend of the new president—so more than a dozen people crowded the little kitchen as I started prepping for dinner. They were eager to see what the fancy chef would come up with, and they were about to be thoroughly disappointed.

That night, the president and his family had about ten minutes to eat before they were whisked off to the many inauguration balls. So I put together a pared-down version of the kind of food I would cook for them for the next six years—food that occupied the place where good flavor overlaps with good-for-you. By the time I had prepared four plates of roasted chicken brushed with barbecue sauce, broccoli with garlic, and brown rice, the onlookers had gone in search of something, anything, more interesting. That was OK by me. I left the White House both excited and wary, because I knew that after the celebration, the time for dreaming was done. What mattered now was making change.

★

THE POLITICAL CLIMATE WASN'T EXACTLY FAVORABLE to our plans. Despite the president's decisive electoral victory, his antagonists in Congress had all but promised to oppose any measure he supported. Not to mention that he took office in the midst of a recession, when slowing the economic freefall seemed more pressing than improving school lunches. Yet the First Lady and I knew that halting the escalating epidemics of diabetes and childhood obesity was just as essential for the success of the nation.

MICHELLE ANNOUNCING THE CHEFS MOVE TO SCHOOLS PROGRAM

From day one until she left the White House, Michelle's sleeves were rolled up and she was absolutely determined to figure out how to improve the health of kids. For the next six years, we would work side by side, and for six years, she would be my daily inspiration. She taught me to ignore the spotlight of Washington and focus on the humbling opportunity we had to help families feed their kids better food, to never get lost in the abstraction of stats, large numbers, and ideology, and to always remember the people affected by policy. Working with her is the greatest honor I've had and probably ever will have.

We expanded our mission to help all Americans eat better. And once again, I stood in awe of the power of regular people.

The first thing we did was plant a vegetable garden. Today, almost a decade later, the garden seems like no big deal. But when we suggested tearing up a thousand or so square feet of the South Lawn of the White House to make way for plots of broccoli, sugar snap peas, and parsley, we were uprooting more than just pristine grass. We were taking radical action and breaking new ground—literally—to make a statement. We got a lot of flak and pushback for it. But we knew how important it was to start a national conversation about the way we eat.

We also set out to understand the issues most important to families as well as identify the areas where we could have the most impact. To do this, we hit upon a simple solution: Listen to what families are saying. Michelle hosted roundtables with parents. She spoke to kids during our many school visits. We dug into opinion polls and consumer behavior reports. We spoke to parents, teachers, community leaders, kids themselves, and every expert we could find to identify the greatest needs and the biggest opportunities for real change. Then we laid out the strategy for how we thought we could help families raise healthier kids. The first major opportunity was in schools. We learned that parents—close to 90 percent of them, according to polls—wanted to improve the nutrition in lunches provided by public schools across the country. Here, in a single piece of legislation, was a chance to affect the health of 31 million children.

The politics weren't pretty—they never are—but we worked out a bill that, among other things, empowered the U.S. Department of Agriculture (USDA) to set new standards for the food that our schools feed our children. These standards effectively lowered lunches' sodium and saturated fat content and increased the amount of fruits, vegetables, and whole grains. They also removed junk foods like candy and soda from cafeterias and vending machines. A lot of people deserve credit for passing the bill: Advocacy groups helped organize and pressure Congress. The First Lady, in an historically bold effort, worked the phones to convince legislators, one by one, to make this bill a priority at a time when there were so many other priorities. She convinced the president, too. As he said at the bill's signing, "Not only am I very proud of the bill, but had I not been able to get this passed, I would be sleeping on the couch." And of course the president deserves credit for risking precious political capital to support the bill. There's a great photo of the president with his hand on the shoulder of Eric Cantor, then the Republican majority whip. At the time they were in the middle of budget negotiations, and looking at the picture, you'd think they were discussing the prospect of a government shutdown. But really, the president was talking to him about our bill. And Cantor ultimately let the bill come up for a vote, enabling it to pass. But without the guidance of the American people, none of it would have happened. Not only did they inform the legislation, but their support was the reason politicians could prioritize it even in the midst of economic turmoil.

Next, we expanded our mission to help all Americans eat better. And once again, I stood in awe of the power of regular people. I met with the biggest players in the food industry, whom most food activists had written off as villains. It's true that many companies had put profits ahead of the well-being of Americans and gravely undermined our health in the process. And we confronted and battled many food companies whose practices were hurting the health of families. But like it or not, you can't fix the food system without engaging those responsible for producing the vast majority of the food we eat. After all, businesses, not governments, feed people. What I learned through this was that the choices we make really do matter, even though it can be easy to imagine they don't.

The idea of regular people swaying companies like Walmart might seem impossible. Yet make no mistake: These companies are listening to us. Each purchase we make is captured, aggregated, and studied in a relentless effort to determine what we want. And during the past decade, we've told them—and they've been scrambling. As Americans bought much less soda and juice, cereal, fast food, and frozen dinners, these big companies became increasingly desperate to figure out what people want instead, which is better access to healthy, convenient food at better prices.

So at the White House, we pressured and prodded food-sector giants to help them make the right changes, changes that would truly improve the health and well-being of Americans. Ultimately, we were more successful than we could've imagined. Walmart was just one example. When the company agreed to lower the price of the fruits and vegetables it sold, to cut the sugar and sodium content of its packaged foods, and to open hundreds of locations in food deserts around the country, we knew that we'd helped make eating better a little easier for nearly half the country.

Victories like these taught me an important lesson that I carried with me throughout my six years at the White House. For the most part, both government and businesses are followers, not leaders. What I came to understand, both in the halls of polit-

Cannellini Beans
White Beans
Garbanzo Beans
BUSH'S BEST
Garbanzos
Chick Peas
FAMILY FAVORITE Recipes
High in Fiber
S KTCHNS CANNELLINI BEANS
1.69
S KTCHNS WHITE BEANS
1.69
S KTCHNS GARBANZO BEANS
1.69
White Beans
Frijoles Blancos
Cannellini Beans
White Kidney Beans
Reduced Sodium
CANNELLINI BEANS
PINTO BEANS
Frijoles Pintos
Dark Red
Kidney Beans
Frijoles Rojos Oscuros
BUSHS BEST CANNELLINI BEANS
1.99
BUSH BEANS CANNELLINI REDUCED SODIUM
1.99
BUSHS BEST KIDNEY BEANS DARK RED
1.99
Club Price!
10/10.00
Thru Tue. Sep. 20
Seasoned Recipe
Frijoles Negros Condimentados
BLACK BEANS
Black Beans
Frijoles Negros
KIDNEY BEANS
Black Beans
with Garlic, Onion & Spices
BUSHS BEST BEANS BLACK
1.99
BUSHS BEST BLACK BEANS REDUCED SODIUM
1.99
BUSHS BEST KIDNEY BEANS REDUCED SODIUM
1.99
S KTCHNS BLACK BEANS SEASONED
1.69
Pinto Beans
Frijoles Pintos
Chili Beans
Pinto Beans
MILD CHILI SAUCE
O organics
organic
Red Kidney Beans
Pinto Beans
Chili Beans
in sauce

ical power and at the negotiating table with billion-dollar companies, was not the awesome authority of the executive branch or the eternal dominance of McDonald's, but the surprising power of the choices we make.

EAT BETTER, NOT "RIGHT"

Working on the front lines of food politics, I came to an important conclusion about how to make real progress on the challenges facing our health and our planet. And it's probably not what you think.

Whether you live in Des Moines or San Francisco, I bet you're familiar with the prescriptions tossed around by certain advocates for healthy, sustainable eating. For these diehards, the only solution to our woes is nothing short of a revolution in the way we eat. "To change food, we must change everything!" many cry. Everyone must eat seasonal, local, organic, biodynamic, and GMO-free heirloom foods, and anything short is a cardinal sin. If they're right, we're screwed. So it's a good thing they're not.

I'll admit that before I got to the White House, I had some similar utopian fantasies. But actually doing the work of policy making—where solutions must work for the many, not the few—quickly forced me out of the bubble of idealism. I came to see that my fellow advocates and I had failed by promoting an impossible standard. We set the bar so high that not even we could reach it. Not too long ago I had lunch with a crusader who had advocated far and wide for avoiding meat and dairy in all meals but dinner. He ordered a pastrami sandwich—with a shmear of chopped chicken liver. If perfection is the enemy of progress, then so is pretense.

So let's ditch both. *No one*—and definitely not me—eats only healthy, sustainable meals. And that's OK. And not all companies that produce a lot of food are bad—it takes an enormous amount of food to feed our country and the world. Yes, we have to make some changes to eat our way toward a food system that's not degrading our health and the environment—but if there's one thing I can say to you, it's that it's vital to think of this goal as a process, a road we travel step by step, meal by meal. If we only look to make dramatic change, we'll find ourselves standing still forever. So let's redefine what it looks like to move forward.

Here's what we know about the challenges we face. After decades of faulty advice on nutrition—the notion that fat was the sole culprit of our health woes, for instance, or more generally, the misguided emphasis on individual nutrients rather than the foods that contain them—we finally have a clear consensus on what makes a healthy diet. Essentially, eat a lot of fruits, vegetables, beans and whole grains, and not a lot of meat or processed foods. I bet you've heard that before. Many people have said it in many ways. And while what's optimal for each person can vary depending on his or her body, in general, this issue truly is as settled as the science on global warming.

We finally have a clear consensus on what makes a healthy diet.

Following more or less that same advice will also help our planet. When you eat a lot of vegetables and fruits, you support crops that release far fewer greenhouse gases during production than animal proteins, which we produce far too much of. When you eat a lot of different whole grains and beans, you support crops that repair our soil, giving us vegetables that grow better, taste better, and are better for us. (And this kind of progress propels itself: The more we demand these foods, the cheaper they get and the easier it is to buy even more of them.) When you swap just a little bit of your beef intake for fish, chicken, or even pork, you're helping to rein in the biggest contributor to carbon emissions in the entire food system.

The data shows that, as a society, we've definitely started to follow this advice, but we need to step up our game. As climate change accelerates, we're going to see harder storms, longer droughts, summer cold streaks, and warmer winters. This is making growing good stuff like produce more difficult and therefore more expensive—and these foods are already out of reach for too many. In other words, unless we do something, it's going to get much harder to eat nutritious food. So if you still need a reason to care about climate change, here it is: It's going to impact your health.

Luckily, "doing something" is possible—and effective. Take a look at what's happened in the past few years when regular people made a few new choices at the store. One day, a soda company drops aspartame from its diet soda. The next, a cereal brand stops using artificial colors and flavors. The next, fast-food chains start reducing sodium content. These might not be the most important changes—artificial colors were never the worst thing about breakfast cereals—but they represent a move in the right direction and should be seen as evidence of your power.

This cookbook is my idea for what the next level of change looks like and how we can achieve it. In this vision, all steps in the right direction are meaningful, and there's a place for everyone. You won't find screeds against government subsidies or dissections of industrial agriculture. (I have plenty to say on the subject of food policy, but that's for another, much less tasty book than this one!) Instead, you'll find practical, pretense-free ideas for what we can all do, buy, cook, and eat *right now*. I'll also offer straightforward explanations of how those choices connect to some of the broader issues we face.

The truth is, you're already having an impact on food policy and our food system. Because whether you know it or not, your choices are already influencing businesses' decisions and government policy. With just a little information and some simple strategies, you can ensure the difference you make is a positive one. If you decide to plant a garden, start composting, or read a food policy book, that's awesome. If you bake spelt bread, make pickles, and shop at farmer's markets, that's awesome, too. But know that even if you don't do any of these things, you can still be part of making change just by putting that box of sugary cereal on a higher shelf and setting a bowl of fruit on your counter.

To improve our health and help save our planet, we don't *have to eat "healthy." We* don't *have to eat sustainably. We* don't *have to eat "right."*

★

SINCE WE HAVE A PRETTY GOOD IDEA OF *WHAT* WE need to do, this book sets out to tackle the real challenge: *how* we actually do it. It begins with a simple idea: To improve our health and help preserve our planet, we *don't* have to eat "healthy." We *don't* have to eat sustainably. We *don't* have to eat "right." But we do have to eat a little better.

Eating better is this cookbook's guiding philosophy. Eating better means making small changes that have a real impact. Eating better means taking a few steps forward without stressing too much about getting all the way there. Eating better means setting reasonable expectations and meeting them. Eating better means that all of us—no matter your starting point—can take this journey together. After all, if we hope to make real progress, we all have a part to play.

So how do you eat better? Well, here's my take: Eat one more vegetable a day. Just one. Eat whole grains and beans once more a week. Eat beef just one fewer time this week. When this becomes your new normal—in two weeks, ten weeks, or a year—you raise the bar again. Even if you close this book right now, you already have all the information you need to improve your health. And if enough people follow suit, we'll see a measurable effect on our planet.

But if you do read on, you'll find a book full of strategies meant to help you take these steps forward. First, I guide you through the same pantry makeover I gave the Obamas, and provide tips on navigating the supermarket and other simple, effective strategies designed to make it easier to eat better.

Next, I share my take on the most common choices we confront as eaters. Do you prioritize buying organic produce, local produce, or simply more produce? Should you buy farmed or wild fish? What concessions can you make to convenience while still joining the march forward? You won't get any lecturing or shaming. Just my no-bull take, plus advice that'll cut through the information clutter that has complicated our relatively simple task.

Finally, there are the recipes. They'll disappoint anyone expecting tips on making flaxseed smoothies or dishes fit for a state dinner. I'm not a health nut or a great chef. I'm a good cook. All I promise is the kind of simple, delicious food I made for the president and his family—the same food I make for mine. Not only will the recipes give you food that tastes great and reflects smart choices—ones that will improve your health and the environment—but they also provide tools, tips, and techniques you can use whenever you cook, whether it's one of my recipes or a dish you're just throwing together from whatever you have on hand.

My hope is that you cook some of these recipes.

But I'd be as happy if you just embrace the spirit of this book: that we all can and should do a little better. You might not always succeed; you might eat a Twinkie or a pile of chicken wings. If you do, it's all right. I fall off the wagon plenty. Occasionally, I eat corn-fed steak, which represents just about everything I stand against. I know it's not a great decision. I also know it's delicious. I do eat it, but sparingly. And the next day, I just try to eat a little better than I did the day before.

HOW TO EAT BETTER (NO WILLPOWER NECESSARY)

Ten years or so ago, we seemed to be on the verge of a new era of smarter eating. The country learned we were all eating too much processed food and too few real foods. To be sure, there have been real signs of progress—for instance, we're drinking much less soda and sugar-laden fruit juice than we did a decade ago. But we have a long long way to go. Our consumption of hyper-processed foods has held more or less steady over the past decade. We still eat only about 40 percent of the fruit and 60 percent of the vegetables that we should be. While calorie consumption has finally dipped after a forty-year surge (or more—that's only as far back as the federal government has been tracking the data), we're still eating way too much.

So we need to focus on *how* to eat more of what we want and less of what we don't. And we need to focus on the simple, easy practices that work, rather than outdated notions that don't—like the idea that eating well is really just all about willpower. Unhealthy eating, the thinking goes, is for the weak who can't resist the chips on the counter. Well, it turns out none of us can, really.

WE EAT WHAT WE SEE

Our fridges and pantries are ground zero for the simple changes that can make a major impact—even when you're hoping to move into the most famous home in America.

When Michelle Obama asked me to give her pantry a makeover during her husband's campaign in 2007, I undertook the mission with her daughters, Sasha and Malia. At the time, their shelves looked like those in most American homes. There was good food and then there were the typical convenience foods we all know and love: salty snacks, sweets, and so-called fruit juice packed with sugar. They had been trying to eat well, but with all of those unhealthy options nearby, the task was virtually impossible. We went through it all, inspecting the ingredients. We set aside any package that listed sugar in any of its many forms—high-fructose corn syrup, fruit juice concentrate, cane sugar, and so on—as one of the first few ingredients, or that contained a bunch of stuff they couldn't pronounce. We were going to pare down and focus on the real food. Real food has nutrition. Fake food doesn't. I wanted them to know what to eat, not just what to avoid.

For the most part, they had fun with the task, reading the ingredients out loud—"Hydrodextromal . . . nope!" (They especially liked when they got to axe some of Mom's favorite foods.)

The foods we kept, we reorganized. We took the fruit out of the bin at the bottom of the fridge and put it in a bowl on the counter. I bought some glass jars, filled them with healthy snacks like almonds, cashews, peanuts, dried cranberries, and dried mango, and put them where the girls could see them. I lined the fridge with clear, easy-to-see containers of carrot sticks, sliced cucumbers, celery, and hummus. We put cookies and brownies—yes, some treats absolutely survived our purge—on the cabinet's top shelf. They might not have been healthy, but at least they were real food, with ingredients limited to things like butter, flour, and chocolate.

To me, these changes were common sense. If you're hungry and you see a banana, that's what you'll grab. If you have to get a stool to reach the brownies, you'll be less likely to indulge—you'll eat it when you *want* it, rather than when you *see* it. And I saw this in action whenever the girls came home from school and rushed into the kitchen while I was prepping dinner. As they rumbled through—"Hi, Sam!"—they grabbed whatever I'd put in the bowl of fruit. And then—"Bye, Sam!"—they rushed off. They wanted a quick snack. *Any* snack, not specifically fruit or cookies. They grabbed what they saw.

I'd figured those small changes I'd suggested for the Obamas might help a little. But once Michelle and I began to dig into the data in the run-up to her Let's Move campaign, it was clear I'd stumbled upon advice with powerful effects. To understand why, consider the incredibly well-funded research that enables supermarkets to so effectively sell us their products. While the marketing strategies vary—displaying products in end-of-aisles; flaunting impulse items near checkout counters; sticking milk at the back of the store so you have to walk down other aisles to find it—they pretty much all rely on a fundamental principle of what behavioral scientists call "choice architecture." Basically: You buy what you see. This might sound obvious. But the effects are significant. In one well-regarded study, simply moving soda from the center of an aisle to the end, where it was more visible, increased sales by more than 50 percent. As numerous studies show, the same is true at home—where you place food has a major impact on how much of it you eat.

We considered, too, our evolving understanding of willpower. Back in the day, we thought strong willpower was what separated the healthy eaters from the rest of us. But, today psychologists and researchers understand that willpower is actually more like a muscle that can get fatigued than a permanent character trait. Because we make so many decisions each day, we make most of them in a flash, almost automatically. Putting thought into each one just isn't possible. Nor is fighting yourself every time you're hungry, which is what relying on willpower alone requires. That's why, when it comes to eating, "we eat what we see" is *the* principle that governs many of our decisions. Just like what Malia and Sasha did when they zipped in and out of the kitchen. This simple truth might be the most important lesson in this book. If you want to eat better, the key isn't trying to be mindful about every decision you make. It's acknowledging that you *can't* be. Instead, it's about setting yourself up for success. You want to do a little planning that allows you to eat well without working for it. It's making sure the stuff you see is good stuff.

If the only action you take is swapping the cookies on your counter for something better, then you will make progress. Realizing that we eat what we see has other implications too. How many times have you actually been full, but kept staring at the platter of fried chicken on the table until you just went for that last piece, and regretted it later? (I'm speaking from experience.)

Well, the same effect happens to some degree every time we set food out in front of us. So there's

an easy way to combat that: just keep the food somewhere else. At dinner at home, you can bring the platter of food back to the counter after everyone's served themselves, and encourage them to go get seconds there if they want.

Or go even one level further, and use smaller plates or bowls when eating. You'll naturally take smaller portions to fit on a smaller plate. And you certainly don't have to deny yourself seconds. It's just that those seconds (or thirds) aren't already on your plate to begin with, so you're less likely to eat them just because they're there.

The takeaway is this: Our food environment plays a major role in the decisions we make. If we improve that environment, we improve those decisions. Make the better choice the easiest choice.

START WITH A (TINY) MAKEOVER

STEP 1: PURGE YOUR PANTRY AND FRIDGE Grab a big bag, go through the food in your kitchen, and toss in any canned, jarred, or boxed products that list any form of sugar—from cane sugar to fruit concentrate to corn syrup—as the first or second ingredient (especially if it's in food where you don't expect to see it, like peanut butter or salad dressing). Bag any product with a long list of ingredients that a sixth grader couldn't pronounce. It's not that some sugar or food additives here and there will kill you. It's that products loaded with them tend to lack nutritional value. The purpose isn't necessarily figuring out what to avoid so much as making sure your home is filled with nutritious food. In the past, I would have then recommended you throw that bag out, but as I've grown to see the huge problems with food *waste*, I now suggest you put that bag in a corner of your pantry, eat what's in it, and just replace each thing with a better option . . . or not at all.

But wait! Don't go too crazy. You have to keep a few treats. If you ask me, it's healthy to have some unhealthy food around. The whole idea behind the pantry purge is to set up a zone in your home where you can eat without worry and guilt. Chips might not be good for you, but neither is stressing out about every bite of food. So make some progress, and indulge once in a while—just make sure it's actually once in a while. Just choose treats you really, really like so that the splurge is worth it, and make sure they don't contain lots of junk.

STEP 2: REORGANIZE YOUR PANTRY Now that you've cleaned house, rearrange what you've kept. Remember, you eat what you see. So first, take those treats you saved and put them on the top shelf (and even better, in a paper bag or another container you can't see through). Put smarter options front and center on shelves at eye level.

Now, put a big bowl of fruit on your counter. Fill large, clear containers with roasted nuts (salted or not) and dried fruit, and keep them on the counter, too. These are real foods that you can feel good about eating. Fresh and dried fruit satisfies sweet cravings without added sugar. Nuts taste rich from good fats and have satisfying protein. They satiate you in a way junk foods don't. And you'll eat them more often when they're on display.

STEP 3: REORGANIZE YOUR FRIDGE Now apply the eat-what-you-see principle to your fridge. The bottom bin might be called the crisper, but it's really more like a cave where fruits and vegetables go to die. I say use it to store condiments, and put those good-for-you foods where you can see them—at eye level if possible. Not only does this improve our eating habits, but it also reduces waste, as anyone who has discovered a forgotten, melting bag of spinach or fuzzy bunch of fruit knows too well.

Even better, make these wholesome foods easier to eat. Take the time to wash and cut ready-to-eat vegetables, like carrots, cucumber, celery, bell peppers, and radishes—and fruit that requires prep, like melon and pineapple—and keep them in clear containers in your fridge. If necessary, stock some dips to make the vegetables more enticing, whether you make Chipotle-Lime Aïoli (page 96) or another recipe from this book (pages 94–99), or buy a dip that would survive the pantry purge.

LEAVE THE STRESS AT THE STORE (AND HOW TO SHOP WITH LESS STRESS)

My plan to help you eat better is all about surrounding your family with food you can feel good about eating. When it comes to food, your home should be a stress-free place, a sanctuary where you can pretty much eat whatever you want, because you've stocked your cabinet and fridge with good stuff. Again, you shouldn't have to rely on willpower and live in a war zone where you wage daily combat against temptation. Don't get me wrong, there is a battle to be fought. But it should go down at the supermarket.

Moving the frontline to the supermarket means you're not under siege in your home. Instead of an endless struggle, you spend only an hour or two per week on guard. I've spent my fair share of time wandering the aisles, making decisions on the fly and filling up my place with unhealthy foods (my weaknesses include ice cream and tortilla chips) that I'd later find myself struggling to resist after a long day. Once I delved into the research on consumer behavior, I saw that I was entering a battle I was sure to lose. You know how I said before that, at home, we eat what we see? Well, at the supermarket, we buy what we see.

Big companies know this. In fact, it's essential to their business model. Between supermarket chains and food manufacturers, hundreds of millions of dollars every year fund research and technology devoted to decoding your buying habits. It might seem like something from a movie about a dystopian future, but it's real: Cameras throughout each store track your path through the aisles and connect these movements to what you buy at checkout. With this kind of data for tens of thousands of people, patterns emerge that reveal how to arrange the products on shelves to maximize what you buy.

It's no accident that sugary drinks and chips are often located at eye level or on endcaps (industry lingo for the highly noticeable front-facing shelves at the end of each aisle). It's no mistake that kids' cereals are placed low so their target audience has a convenient view of the cartoon characters on the boxes. The companies that make these products actually pay a premium to stores for prime shelf space, because they know they'll sell more of their high-profit items. Everyone wins—except the customer. Higher-profit items tend to be made with the cheapest ingredients, and the cheapest ingredients (like sugar, salt, oil) tend to be the least nutritious. The effectiveness of these tactics is one of the reasons we all eat so much of this stuff.

The good news is that savvy marketing is no match for a knowledgeable customer. Just knowing their tricks helps you withstand them. Here's what I suggest (and do):

- Before you even get to the grocery store, make a plan. Spending just ten minutes writing a list of what you need makes you less likely to wander and make the sort of impulse purchases that marketing strategies rely on. Of course, you can be flexible—if a vegetable or cut of meat looks great or is on sale, give yourself leeway to ponder and get inspired for dinner. But for the most part, stick to your plan and push your cart purposefully through the aisles.

- Have a snack. Really! Eating a satisfying snack before shopping means you won't hit the store hungry, which makes the task of resisting temptation easier.

- Don't linger in the aisles full of the least healthy options like cereal, chips, and cookies. I don't know about you, but the more time I spend bombarded by sweet, salty, crunchy snacks, the more likely I am to crack.

vermont creamery
ORGANIC
Chicken Broth

Raisin Nut Bran
NEW!
WHOLE GRAIN
Post
HONEY BUNCHES OF OATS
Whole Grain
HONEY CRUNCH
NEW!
Kellogg's
Mini Wheats
HARVEST Delights
NEW!
Kellogg's
Mini Wheats
HARVEST Delights
Blueberry
Post
Raisin Bran
HUNDREDS OF RAISINS IN EVERY BOX
Post
HONEY BUNCHES OF OATS
HONEY ROASTED
Oats & More with Honey
BUY this box HELP GIVE a child breakfast
Kellogg's
Raisin Bran
Kellogg's
Raisin Bran
DEDICATED
Post
QUAKER
life
Now MORE Clusters!
Kellogg's
Raisin Bran
Crunch

WHAT ACTUALLY MATTERS

For many people, buying something as basic as tomatoes has become an exercise in self-doubt. The organic beauties are tempting, but they're twice the price of conventional tomatoes and have been shipped in from Mexico. Plus, it's February—isn't it some sort of culinary sin to eat a tomato in the winter? Virtually every purchase is full of contradictions. Is cheese a great source of protein or a worrisome source of fat? Is fruit full of vitamins or full of sugar? Is bread vital sustenance or the root of all evil? It's enough to make you throw up your hands and eat a cheeseburger.

When you're the public face of the White House's food and nutrition policy, you get these kinds of questions from everyone from college buddies to congressmen. (You hear a lot of confessions, too. "I was really bad last night," some TV pundit or senior staffer would whisper, telling me of tubs of ice cream consumed, fast food ordered, and diets broken.) At parties and meetings, people would ask me about their shopping decisions, looking for my thumbs-up in the same way you'd ask a doctor friend about the mole on your left calf.

I want to share with you what I did with them, beginning now with perhaps the most important piece of advice: Take a deep breath. Let's stop trying to making perfect choices and focus on making good ones. Let's be conscious of, but not obsessed with, what we eat. Then the stress will melt away, like butter on hot toast.

Ideally we'd all shop at the edges of the store, where the fresh produce lives, and never buy food in a box. We'd bake our own bread, make our own pickles, and mix up our own granola. But everyone has to go down the center aisles for staples like cooking oil and canned tomatoes. The truth is, we're going to buy some food that's been processed, either highly or mildly. When you do, you just want to be able to choose the better option. How to do it can seem overwhelming, unless you focus your energy on what matters.

Take the Food and Drug Administration's Nutrition Facts label, which you see on the back of every jar, box, and bag at the grocery store. This tidy black-and-white rectangle tells you a lot: the serving size, servings per container, calories, total fat, saturated fat, cholesterol, sodium, carbohydrates, fiber, and protein, as well as the amount of various vitamins and minerals. At first glance, it seems like a good thing to know so much about the food you eat. Yet when we reached out to regular Americans—in other words, those who didn't think about protein and fiber for a living—we learned that all this information wasn't empowering. It was confusing. The sheer amount of data obscured the stuff that really told you whether a particular product was good for you. We fought with some success to change the label. Yet if it were up to me alone, I would've scrapped 75 percent of it. Fortunately, this book doesn't require congressional approval.

The same glut of information that afflicts the Nutrition Facts label has complicated the straightforward task of eating well, and it's keeping us all stuck in place. In theory, the more information we have, the more informed our choices should be. But in reality, too much can cause a sort of paralysis. Psychologists call the phenomenon "information overload"—perhaps more appropriate for this book, it sometimes goes by the term "infobesity"—and research shows that it causes poor decision making and anxiety. No wonder that even though more of us than ever report that we're trying to eat healthy, for the most part, despite some encouraging signs of progress, we're not.

In the interest of simplifying the task of eating better than you did yesterday, let's cut through the information clutter to focus on the stuff that deserves your attention and to provide clear-cut answers to common questions that come up as you shop.

SHOULD I AVOID SUGAR?

We've all heard it before—we're eating way too much sugar and it's literally killing us. But before you get caught up in "good sugar" versus "bad sugar," think of it this way: Consider the source of the sugar. By that, I mean that the culprit is *not* the sugar that occurs naturally in whole vegetables and fruits. These foods come bearing nutrients. They also contain fiber (note that fruit juice, however, does *not*), which among other things helps slow the rate at which your body absorbs their sugar. And yep, that's good! Fruits and vegetables are foods you want to eat more of, not less. And they'll generally fill you up before you overdo it. The problem is *added* sugar, which is why, at the White House, we included it as a new category on the Nutrition Facts label. Added sugar will appear where you'd expect it—at least you know what you're getting with cookies and cake—and also where you might not, like bread, tomato sauce, and salad dressing. So eat fewer sweet treats, and avoid products that contain added sugars. This advice holds no matter what form the added sugar takes, whether it's high-fructose corn syrup (the villain of the moment) or one of the dozens of other sugar synonyms—yes, including virtuous-sounding ones like cane sugar, fruit concentrate, agave syrup, and honey.

WHAT ABOUT ARTIFICIAL SWEETENERS?

The best you can do is choose drinks like water and unsweetened tea over sugar-laden ones. That's the easy answer, because, of course, we don't always make the best choice. There are a lot of questions surrounding artificial sweeteners. Despite what you might have heard, they're not really unsafe—you'd have to drink many cases of diet soda a day to approach toxic levels of saccharine, aspartame, or sucralose. I don't advise doing that, just as I'd suggest you avoid eating a hundred gallons of rice for dinner (about the amount necessary for trace amounts of arsenic in the grain to hurt you). If you're struggling to kick a sweet-drink habit, switching to low- or no-calorie drinks beats guzzling those sweetened with lots of sugar. But here's where things admittedly get a little tricky: Emerging evidence suggests that synthetic sweeteners could actually increase your sugar cravings, since they trick your brain into thinking you're getting sugar, but when your body realizes it doesn't have those ready calories, it may want them more. The science is still new, but it's something to be conscious of. Still, if you go from sugar soda to diet soda as a bridge to unsweetened drinks, that's progress in my book.

WHAT'S UP WITH GOOD FATS AND BAD FATS?

The issue of fats can be a bit confusing. Not long ago, fat was enemy number one—the (faulty) advice was to count fat grams, and everyone worried about it constantly. Now we know there are good fats and not-so-good ones, and even those keep changing, adding another layer of confusion. So instead of worrying about which fats are which, I say butter your bread, spike your coffee with half-and-half, eat nuts, gobble avocado, and drizzle as much olive oil as you want. In other words, cross fat off your list of obsessions, especially if that fat comes from plants or fish. Instead, focus on limiting those mega-calorie meals—you know, the obvious ones: pizza parties, burgers, deep-fried foods, huge portions of greasy stuff. The calories here are typically driven by massive amounts of fat, and typically the "bad" saturated kind.

Whole Chicken
onions
Garlic
tomatoes

SHOULD I AVOID SALT?

Consuming too much sodium (or for all practical purposes, "salt") has a serious effect on our health, mainly by causing high blood pressure and heart disease. That case is closed. And we are eating way too much salt; the average American consumes about 50 percent more than what's recommended. But there's an important distinction to be made: The problem isn't the generous pinch you use to season the chicken you grill or the broccoli you roast. The *real* problem is the salt content of hyper-processed food, or in chain restaurants, where it's used in amounts you'd never use at home. Exactly how much salt is too much is still debated. But this book is about just doing better. And reducing your consumption of hyper-processed foods will reduce the sodium in your diet. When you can't avoid them, choose those with the lowest sodium content.

EAT FIBER, BE HAPPY

Vitamins and minerals get all the credit. But the other big reason fruits, vegetables, whole grains, beans, and legumes are good for you is that they contain the misunderstood, underestimated, decidedly unromantic component known as fiber.

I know, hearing about vitamin A and iron is dull enough, but evoking fiber in a cookbook is the ultimate buzzkill, the equivalent of devoting a spread in an architectural magazine to plumbing. But the truth remains: Eating more fiber should be one of your top priorities.

I don't make this sort of recommendation lightly. For the most part, reducing nutrition to food's individual components is misguided. Virtually every time we've tried to isolate the enemy (fat!) or savior (antioxidants!) of our health, we've been off base. The focus on a single trendy fruit or vitamin or mineral has confused the otherwise straightforward task of eating well. If you eat a good variety of nutrient-dense foods, you don't have to pay attention to the whats or the whys.

But if there's any exception to this rule, it's fiber. It's one of the few cases where the benefits are clear. Still, fewer than 3 percent of Americans get as much of it as they should. Perhaps that's because the role of fiber is so widely misunderstood. While fiber is probably most commonly associated with, well, "regularity," its benefits go way beyond that.

I could go on and on about why. I could talk about how fiber is good for us in a totally different way than other nutrients, how nutrients are absorbed by specialized cells in our gut, how the fiber that's left inside us actually feeds the trillions of friendly bacteria that reside there, known collectively as the microbiome. We're still learning about all the ways a happy microbiome keeps us happy, but already there is a compelling correlation between gut health and better outcomes for asthma, allergies, inflammation, and obesity, to name a few.

Recently, these little friends have received some attention. It's why yogurt brands tout their probiotic qualities and people have been popping probiotic pills and embracing unpasteurized fermented foods like sauerkraut. But if you really want to treat your microscopic buddies nice, my prescription is a familiar one: Eat more fruits and vegetables, which have lots of fiber, and eat more whole grains and legumes, which tend to have even more.

SHOULD I COUNT CALORIES?

In the quest to eat less, keeping tabs on every bite in order to track progress is a reasonable strategy. The problem is, it's stressful and next to impossible to accomplish. A better strategy to reduce calorie consumption is to focus on the quality, not the quantity, of your calories. In other words, don't count calories—make calories count. Empty calories—that is, calories that don't have nutritional value—are the main culprit of our woes. Make sure the food you eat is full of nutrients, and number crunching becomes unnecessary. When your body gets what it needs, you feel satiated and you'll be less likely to overeat.

Of course, this is a strategy, not a guarantee. So while you don't have to count every calorie, you do want to have a basic awareness to help you look for, and help you avoid, extremes. Adults need somewhere around two thousand calories a day, depending on how active they are. So whenever a snack takes up a quarter of that recommended daily intake or a single meal approaches half, think twice about it. Otherwise, relax, enjoy yourself, and don't worry about every bite.

SHOULD I BUY "NATURAL" FOODS?

Don't treat the word "natural" on a product's label as a beacon of health; treat it as marketing gibberish and a big, waving red flag. The minimally regulated term (often confused with the far-better-policed "organic") generally indicates the absence of artificial flavors and synthetic substances in a product, but it doesn't necessarily mean you want to feed that product to your family. Think of it this way: A carrot doesn't have to boast that it's natural. Products that do tend to have something to prove. They're often highly processed and too far removed from whole foods to contain much nutrient value, so take an especially close look at the list of ingredients to make sure you're not buying just another snack loaded with some version of sugar. (And looking for fiber on the nutrition label isn't a bad idea—see opposite.)

ARE FOOD ADDITIVES GOING TO KILL ME?

There's good reason to avoid products with a bunch of additives—the often unpronounceable ingredients added to preserve, color, thicken, or otherwise alter a food's natural state—but not because they're radioactive. While it's true that additives don't receive the long-term study they should, what additive-packed products contain is less important than what they don't. Whether you're talking about sugar, soy lecithin, or FD&C Blue No. 1, the presence of additives often indicates food without much nutritional value—the very definition of "not good for you." But let's be realistic. We're going to buy some jarred, boxed, or canned food that contains additives. Canned tomatoes, for instance, usually contain ascorbic acid, a preservative that keeps them from turning brown. Would it be better to use fresh tomatoes in season or preserve your own? Sure. Can you eat store-bought canned tomatoes? Absolutely. So let's set a more reasonable goal. Eat as little processed food as you can. When you do eat it, though, try to choose products whose labels don't list more than a couple of words a sixth grader couldn't pronounce.

ARE GMOS EVIL OR WILL THEY SAVE HUMANITY?

You've probably heard versions of both of these takes on GMOs (genetically modified organisms). Yet as is so often the case, the issue isn't black or white. It's gray. Here's what I know: Although the technology—altering the genetic makeup of plants by implanting genes from other living things—

sounds like the plot of a sci-fi thriller, there isn't a single credible study that shows that GMOs are dangerous to eat. And while genetic modification shows promise as a way to address the challenges of feeding a growing population on a rapidly warming planet, GMOs are no magic bullet. So far, their primary application has been to grow corn and soy more efficiently. These crops mainly end up as feed for livestock and fodder for processed foods, so in that way GMOs reinforce a food system that's not working for us or the environment. And while new gene-editing technologies have the potential to reduce the use of herbicides and fertilizers, and make plants more nutritious and taste better, we are still years off from those foods showing up on shelves.

The problem, then, isn't the tool, but how it's used. As climate change accelerates, food will become much more difficult to grow. Gene-editing technology might help with that, so I think it's wise to keep it as a tool in our toolbox. The topic of GMOs takes up valuable space in the conversation around our food system. We need to keep the fundamental goal of ensuring that all families have access to healthy, affordable, sustainably produced food as the top priority. For now, the best way for you to help to support a more sustainable, diverse food system is by eating more fruits, vegetables, and whole grains. By doing so, you'll largely avoid GMOs. But when you do consume products made with GMOs—and we all do, whether we realize it or not—the sun will still rise the next morning.

WHAT SHOULD I LOOK FOR ON A LABEL?

To figure out whether a product like bread or cereal is worth the stomach space, I take a look at the

Nutrition Facts

Serving Size 2/3 cup (55g)
Servings Per Container About 8

Amount Per Serving	
Calories 230	Calories from Fat 72
	% Daily Value*
Total Fat 8g	**12%**
Saturated Fat 1g	**5%**
Trans Fat 0g	
Cholesterol 0mg	**0%**
Sodium 160mg	**7%**
Total Carbohydrate 37g	**12%**
Dietary Fiber 4g	**16%**
Sugars 1g	
Protein 3g	
Vitamin A	10%
Vitamin C	8%
Calcium	20%
Iron	45%

* Percent Daily Values are based on a 2,000 calorie diet. Your daily value may be higher or lower depending on your calorie needs.

	Calories:	2,000	2,500
Total Fat	Less than	65g	80g
Sat Fat	Less than	20g	25g
Cholesterol	Less than	300mg	300mg
Sodium	Less than	2,400mg	2,400mg
Total Carbohydrate		300g	375g
Dietary Fiber		25g	30g

Nutrition Facts label and zoom in on fiber. Spotting more than 3 grams per serving of bread and 6 grams per serving of cereal is a solid, if imperfect, indicator that the food is good for you. Because while fiber isn't sexy, it's vastly more important than its reputation suggests. (See the sidebar "Eat Fiber, Be Happy," on page 38.) Then check the label to see if the serving size and calories are reasonable, and be a little skeptical if there are lots of sodium, sugars, or saturated fat. Or know that this might be an occasional food.

COOK A LITTLE MORE

Look, I know it's hard. Like, really hard. You get home late from work, you're tired, the kids are hungry. And I know that people in my position throw around the advice (or command) "Cook more!" like it's easy, as if our lives are set up for spending a couple hours every night cooking.

Still, bear with me here, because cooking at home *is* one of the best things you can do for your family's well-being. And to help, most of the recipes in this book are designed to make it easier to do so, whether you cook at home every night, or just once more a week. Now, this is where you might expect me to wax poetic on the ritual of eating together and the importance of spending time with the people you love. And yes, dinner was when my parents bugged me about getting my homework done and talked about politics, culture, and life. And yes, I was especially moved to see the president of the United States make time to eat with his wife and kids practically every night.

The data shows that when families cook and eat together, everything gets better. **Everything.**

Yet it was the *measurable* effect of eating together as a family—and eating food cooked at home—that grabbed me. Not only is cooking typically less expensive than eating out or ordering in, but virtually every meal you cook at home will be better for you. For the most part, restaurants serve dishes meant to please, not to nourish. And that's OK. A little indulgence is good, as long as you realize you're indulging. At home, few of us engage in the eating habits restaurants encourage. I don't know about you, but I don't usually deep-fry in my apartment, or eat two courses followed by a slab of chocolate cake. When you're doing the cooking, you can relax, employing salt and even butter liberally, knowing common sense will act as a guardrail to extreme eating. (Remember when Alois wanted me to hit that sauce with a metric ton of butter? That doesn't happen at home.)

So cook as much as your life allows. Cook one more meal each week and eat it around the table with your family. Don't take it from me: The data shows that when families cook and eat together, everything gets better. *Everything.* Not only do they consume more fruits, vegetables, and whole grains and less salt, sugar, and calories, but kids' behavior improves, grades go up, and even drug use and teen pregnancy dip.

OOSE
PA

WASTE LESS

A couple years back, I got together with Dan Barber, the pioneering New York chef behind Blue Hill at Stone Barns, to cook lunch, and I don't think I've ever been so nervous. This was partly because of whom we were cooking for—a collection of more than forty world leaders, mostly heads of state—and partly because of what we were cooking.

The then-secretary general of the UN, Ban Ki-moon, had assembled this formidable bunch about a month before the 2015 Climate Change Conference in Paris as a sort of pregame to the summit ahead. Most chefs in their right mind would take this opportunity to show off their most impressive techniques and the finest ingredients. But we were serving food that had been headed for the garbage.

We served presidents from China to France "landfill salad" (made from produce scraps and rejects) and a burger with a patty fashioned from the pulp left over from juicing vegetables. I admit, for a moment I wondered what the hell we'd been thinking.

Every morning, you wake up, open the fridge, and set four dollar bills on fire.

Luckily, Dan and his team did the heavy lifting, from dreaming up the dishes to gathering the raw materials, a tough task since there's still no good system for rescuing useful refuse. In fact, he was the one who gave me the idea in the first place. One of the most articulate and thoughtful chefs on the issue of sustainable agriculture, he'd recently invited fellow chefs to get creative with roots and peels, the leftovers from filleting fish, and other stuff destined for the trash. He was asking us to rethink what we waste. How can it be that we throw away so much that can be made into incredibly delicious food?

Food waste is an area where there's a big problem but also big potential for progress. In the United States, we waste 40 percent of our food.

All that waste affects our climate, too. Every year, more than 50 million tons of food ends up rotting in landfills and releasing methane, a greenhouse gas that traps heat at a much higher rate than carbon dioxide. All told, food waste alone accounts for a whopping 8 percent of global greenhouse gas emissions. If it were a country, food waste would clock in just behind the U.S. and China as the world's third-largest emitter.

Here's another reason to care: Waste affects your bottom line. All the water, fertilizer, and labor that goes into the production and distribution of food that's never eaten increases the price of the food we buy.

While the majority of food waste takes place before you check out at the grocery store, a remarkable 43 percent happens *after*. So picture this: Every morning, you wake up, open the fridge, and set four dollar bills on fire.

This is essentially what every American family does, on average throwing out $1,500 worth of food a year. Like everyone else, I know the feeling of discovering a bag of spoiled spinach, a troop of spongy eggplants, or a carton of sour milk. I might've forgotten about them. I might even have been off giving a speech about how much food we waste.

But what we throw away often isn't trash. It's good, flavorful food that just needs a little love.

WHAT YOU CAN DO *TODAY*

No, a head of lettuce sacrificed to the trash isn't the end of the world. No, I'm not about to insist you start hoarding the liquid in canned chickpeas to make vegan mayonnaise and meringues. (Yup, this is a thing.) Hey, more power to those who do. But a few small changes to your routine can make a big difference, helping the planet and saving you money.

BUY WHAT YOU'LL USE

Before you hit the grocery store, take a couple of minutes to make a plan. Even a basic idea of what the week's worth of meals might be—chicken with roasted broccoli on Monday, dinner out with a friend on Tuesday, salmon with vegetables and rice for Wednesday—will help keep your shopping haul more in line with what you'll actually eat. And before you head out, take a look at what you already have in the fridge and pantry so you don't accidentally double up, as I do far too often.

USE WHAT YOU BUY

Afterwards, take a minute to jot down a list of what you bought, so good stuff doesn't get lost to a crowded fridge. Because you eat what you see, keep vegetables, fish, meat, and other foods with short shelf lives in clear containers and in plain sight, preferably at eye level. And plan to eat the things that spoil the quickest first.

RETHINK STALKS, STEMS & LEAVES

There are some incredibly resourceful cooks out there who use every edible scrap in their homes, pickling watermelon rind and stashing vegetable trimmings to make stock, and ending the week with exactly one cup's worth of garbage. That's awesome. I'm not quite so diligent. But I've found that one of the easiest ways to reduce waste at my place is by focusing on the stalks, stems, and leaves so many of us toss without much thought. Whenever you find yourself about to trash half of what you bought, ask yourself, *What am I doing?!*

- Consider the typical bunch of leafy greens like collards or kale. When you strip the leaves, as so many recipes instruct, you're left with a heavy handful of stems. Instead of tossing half the money you spent, thinly slice those stems and sauté them for a few minutes, just until they start to soften, before adding the greens. You're not just doing the planet and your budget a solid, you've added an awesome crisp element and doubled the size of your dish.

- Same goes for vegetables like broccoli and cauliflower. Florets might hog the spotlight, but the thick stalks taste just as good—often sweeter, even. Peel them with a vegetable peeler until there are no more thick white fibers, chop them, and cook them with the florets.

- While you buy beets (and turnips, radishes, carrots, etc.) for the sweet root, bunches often come with a bonus—the tasty leaves and stems. It's a vegetable two-for-one deal. Just cut them off, give them a good rinse or soak to clean them, and sauté them with a little garlic or bacon.

- Some chefs pluck every leaf of parsley or cilantro from the stems. At home, the lazy cook's path is also the wise one: Chop herb stems along with the leaves, discarding only the thick, woody ones.

REVIVE WILTED GREENS

If you have a head of lettuce starting to go limp, or your kale conks out, submerge the leaves in a bowl of cold water and add some ice cubes. In fifteen minutes or so, they'll be back from the brink and great to eat.

DOUBT THOSE DATES

We've all dumped a jar of tomato sauce after seeing that the stamped-on date has passed. Yet those dates, accompanied by terms like "Sell By" or "Best Before," are not standardized, regulated, or really even connected to safety. Instead, they typically represent a best guess by a company about when a product's quality starts to suffer.

OK, so what do you do when you find something that's probably past its prime? Some, including those who have studied the subject, say they'd eat unopened packaged food years after the sell-by date, but they're braver than I am. I favor a middle ground. If something in your fridge is a few days or maybe a couple weeks after the date, give it a careful look or a good sniff. If it looks and smells normal, it's almost certainly fine. Give it a little taste, if you want. And if you still have any doubt, sure, throw it out.

TREAT RECIPES AS GUIDANCE, NOT GOSPEL

As you measure the ¾ cup of broccoli florets or count out the 6 carrots that this or that recipe calls for, keep in mind that the bits you leave behind could end up lost in the fridge. Instead, just add them to whatever you're making. No dinner has ever been ruined by an extra quarter cup of chopped onions.

CLEAR OUT THAT FRIDGE

Despite doing my best to follow my own advice, the reality is that by the end of the week, my fridge frequently contains a strange collection of edible matter. There might be half a cabbage, a few celery sticks, and a bell pepper with crow's feet. Maybe I find a few leftover florets of roasted broccoli or slabs of grilled zucchini. None of it has gone bad but they're part of the unromantic reality of cooking. Making use of them is a key to cutting down on waste. While they may not be pretty, they're still totally delicious and can become a great meal. Here's what I do to make use of these bits:

★ Chop them fairly fine and cook them in a slick of oil or butter with a generous pinch of salt over medium heat until they're soft and sweet.

- ☆ Toss the sautéed vegetables with simply cooked beans (page 264), lentils (page 270), or whole grains (pages 230, 236, 240, 246, 252, and 259).
- ☆ Add them to tomatoes and leftover pork shoulder to make ragu for pasta (page 202).
- ☆ Stir the sautéed bits into Farro Risotto (page 241) a minute or so before it's ready.
- ☆ Blend them with water or stock and use them as the base for bean soup (page 204) or lentil soup (page 273).

★ Thinly slice the leftovers and cook them in a slick of oil with a generous pinch of salt over high heat until tender with a slight crunch.

- ☆ Substitute the mixture for the vegetables in fried brown rice (pages 233–34).
- ☆ Stir them into Leftover Roasted Chicken Stir-Fry (page 178).

★ Cut leftover raw vegetables into 1-inch pieces, toss them with a splash of oil, and spread them in a roasting pan. Top with a chicken and roast (page 173), so the tasty chicken fat and juices soak them.

HOW TO MAKE A BETTER MEAL

You've got a bowl of fruit and containers of nuts on the counter. You put the chips on a high shelf and chucked the soda. Your fridge and cabinets are full of real food. Already you've set yourself up for success. Now it's time to make dinner. The recipes in this book are here to help. They're here to tempt you with downright deliciousness to eat more vegetables, whole grains, and beans, and to make smart choices about meat and fish. But the question remains—how do you turn good food into a good meal? In other words, what does a healthier, better plate of food look like? (And how do we get it on the table as conveniently as possible?)

The First Lady had the same question. Over plates of catfish, brown rice, and beans at her Chicago home, we talked a lot about how to support families who wanted to make better choices. And at the time, the advice coming from the government certainly wasn't helping. I'm talking about the iconic food pyramid.

In 1991, the USDA released the familiar pyramid, which the agency immediately changed after a meat industry freak-out. As documented by Marion Nestle in her excellent book *Food Politics*, the version released a year later reflected the influence of powerful food interests. It drew deservedly harsh criticism from nutrition advocates who thought that the guidance should perhaps be based on science, not industry lobbying.

Beyond the need for guidance to be science-based, Michelle had an additional, more fundamental objection: The food pyramid just didn't make sense to most people. By 2005, the pyramid had morphed into a triangle broken into bands of different colors and sizes, the base crammed with images of vegetables and fruits, milk and cheese, meat and pasta and bread. Michelle wondered how she—or anyone, for that matter—could possibly use this information to make a healthful plate of food. I couldn't figure it out either, and I've devoted my life to this stuff. We looked at the research and it backed up her feeling: Other parents didn't understand the pyramid either. Between the muddled guidance from the government and the marketing from the food industry, parents just weren't sure what a balanced meal looked like.

So in 2011, we replaced the familiar triangle with MyPlate, an illustration that shows what a healthy plate looks like. The plate is broken into sections—one each for protein, grains, fruits, vegetables, and dairy—whose sizes reflect the ideal proportion. MyPlate is simpler than the food pyramid, and actually communicates *less* information. But it's the *right* information. That's what matters.

Of course, you shouldn't take the plate literally. No one's saying you have to serve a glass of milk alongside dinner, but that the dairy you do use—say, the Parmesan you sprinkle over a salad or the cream you mix into farro risotto—should exist in relatively small proportion to the other food on your plate. No one's saying that every meal must include both fruits *and* vegetables. But if you're making oatmeal (a grain), don't add just a couple of blueberries—add a big handful. If you're grilling zucchini or roasting broccoli or baking sweet potatoes, cook enough so these great-for-you foods make up about half the stuff on your plate.

The recipes in this book are delicious ideas for how to fill each section of that plate with food that represents progress for our health and environment. Sure, not everything on your table will come from this book. When you have the time, consider combining two or three recipes to make dinner. But part of that all-important "how" question is how to make the task of composing a balanced meal doable. So when you're planning a meal but are short on time,

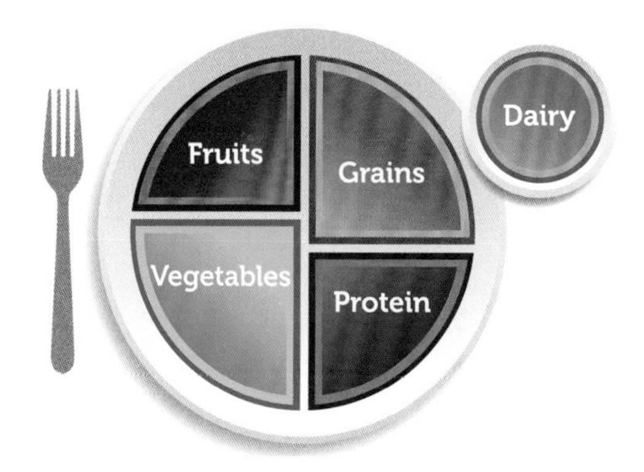

I encourage you to pick just one recipe that tempts you and fill in the blanks with dead-simple preparations. If you're eager to make bulgur salad with pistachios and pomegranate seeds (page 256), serve it with simply baked salmon seasoned with nothing but salt and a pile of spinach with your favorite dressing. If you want to braise pork sausages with bitter greens (page 208), round it out with a bowl of unadorned cooked grains, leaning on the saucy dish for added flavor.

In addition to specific recipes, you'll find guidance for making the sort of unglamorous but delicious dishes that we all rely on to get dinner on the table. I'm talking about advice on cooking fillets of fish (page 140) and chicken breasts (page 193), roasting (page 57) or grilling (page 75) whatever vegetables you have on hand, or making plain-old quinoa (page 236) or bulgur (page 252) or brown rice (page 230).

Make dinner both easy on yourself and delicious for your family. Take comfort in the fact that, even as talk of dieting fads and trendy cure-alls and conflicting nutritional guidance swirls all around you, you can use the basic advice contained in this simple tool to take a step forward. Because if the plate of food you make looks just a little more like the model, you're doing better.

A NOTE ABOUT MEASUREMENTS IN THESE RECIPES (don't sweat them too much)

Most of the food in this book is simple, the kind of stuff I tend to cook at home. But it deserves mentioning that simple food often relies on a little flexibility—something that's hard to account for in recipes, with their tendency toward precise amounts. Not every head of broccoli is the same size. Not every lemon provides the same acidity. Every tomato tastes a little bit different. Even a teaspoon of kosher salt delivers a different level of saltiness depending on the brand. Add to that the fact that we all have different preferences—what's too salty for one person might be just right for another—and you'll see why precision can be, well, a recipe for disappointment. But at the same time, many cooks really *like* being told to add a precise amount of oil, salt, or lemon juice. So I do that in these recipes, but I also encourage flexibility. Instead of a precise amount of salt, I provide a range meant to lead you to a place that's tasty no matter what kind of kosher salt you've got, but you should use the amount that tastes best to you. Same with lemon and lime juice; squeeze on enough to make the dish taste bright and delicious. After all, the goal is more important than the amount. One piece of advice: While you should always trust your own taste, I've found adding a little more acidity—a few drops of vinegar, or a squeeze of citrus—can often lead you to delicious new territory.

EAT MORE VEGETABLES

If you've ever watched TV, you know the drill: Two guys show up at a dull get-together. Then someone shows up with frosty bottles of beer. All of a sudden the scene looks like spring break in Cancun. Everyone's flashing flirty smiles and plenty of skin. Life is a party.

Let me offer a slight change in the script. At my party, the fun doesn't start until someone shows up with a tray of cauliflower roasted and showered with almonds and herbs. LeBron James is shooting threes with apples and oranges. Bryce Harper bench-presses a platter of sweet potatoes. Just then, Beyoncé and Jay-Z materialize, holding mics in one hand and plates of charred zucchini in the other.

You're probably not going to see my version of a good time any time soon, in part because my fellow nutrition advocates continue to think that the best way to push carrots, peppers, and spinach is to sell you vitamin B, calcium, and fiber. Meanwhile, the Don Drapers behind big brands sell love, sex, and happiness. I'll give you one guess at whose strategy moves more product.

So here's what I'll tell you: Vegetables are sent from Mother Nature to make you feel great. Beets are full of love. Broccoli is sexy. And green beans are the key to happiness. Vegetables are beautiful, sweet, crunchy, juicy, and just damn delicious. And oh yeah, they happen to be good for you and the planet, too.

This section of the book is devoted to recipes, techniques, and strategies that will help you eat more vegetables—more kinds, more colors, more often. I'll share my no-recipe-required methods for roasting and grilling vegetables, my two favorite ways to treat them. I'll show you that leaving vegetables raw can make dinner easier but no less delicious. And I go all in on sweet potatoes: They deserve your devotion. The more vegetables we eat, the more vegetables we'll grow. The more we grow, the lower the prices. The lower the prices, the more we'll eat. Call it a delicious cycle.

ORGANIC, SEASONAL, LOCAL, OR NONE OF THE ABOVE

Purists, idealists, and other warriors in the food revolution avert your eyes: Not all Americans shop at farmer's markets.

Look, I love farmer's markets and the holy trinity of perfect eating—food that's local, seasonal, and often organic. But remember, perfect eating is a fantasy for just about everyone.

In real life, I'd wager that you, like me, do most of your shopping at the supermarket. That might be because the supermarket is super convenient, or because there's no farmer's market in your area, or because it's winter and the only things on the folding tables manned by bundled-up vendors are cellared potatoes and turnips. In other words, there are plenty of good reasons why you find yourself buying food in a place where checking all three of those boxes isn't necessarily possible. So you've probably found yourself staring at both organic asparagus shipped from far away and local, seasonal squash grown with fertilizers and pesticides, and wondering whether you're ruining the world either way.

In the quest to both do better and stress out less, let's acknowledge this encouraging truth: As long as you're eating more vegetables—yes, even if they're not organic or are flown in from far away—you're doing better for your health and the planet's.

Organic, local, seasonal—they're great. We should do what we can to promote these qualities, but fetishizing them can have the unintended consequence of discouraging us from eating fruits and vegetables that fall into the "none of the above" category. This is particularly true with organic produce. I've gotten this question more times than I can count: If pesticides and fertilizers are so bad, then shouldn't we avoid them at all costs? The thing is, eating too few fruits and vegetables has serious consequences for our health—far greater than the real but occasionally overblown concerns about not eating organic. As it is, three-quarters of Americans don't eat as many fruits and vegetables as they should. The evidence shows that the single best thing we can do for ourselves, our kids, and our kids' kids is to eat more fruits and vegetables. So yes, buy organic (or seasonal and local) if and when you can. But when you can't, still buy the vegetables.

ROAST THOSE VEGETABLES

YOU NEED DINNER. You have vegetables in the fridge. You're not sure what to do with them. My solution is almost always the same: Roast them. Coated in a slick of oil, hit with a generous sprinkle of salt, and cooked in a hot oven, virtually any vegetable transforms from mild-mannered to thrilling. Roasting intensifies flavor and reveals sides of even familiar vegetables that you didn't realize existed. Take broccoli. Raw, it's pleasant, slightly bitter, and crunchy. Steamed, it's the butt of jokes, at least until butter gets involved. But after you pull a tray of caramelized florets from the oven, the stalks sweet with a soft crunch and the buds salty and crispy, I guarantee no one will be laughing—they'll be too busy eating.

We all know carrots, potatoes, cauliflower, and Brussels sprouts taste great roasted, but there's no need to stop at the usual suspects. You can roast radishes and cabbage, green beans and sugar snap peas, whole scallions, pods of okra, and leaves of kale. While the oven does the work for you, you're free to sauté shrimp, sear pork chops, or put away laundry.

I love eating roasted vegetables with nothing more than salt and lemon. Yet when I'm having friends over, or if the other components of my meal are dead-simple, I like to raise the bar on plain roasted greatness. Turn the page and you'll find recipes for combinations I look to again and again to take vegetables in exciting directions without straying from weeknight-dinner territory.

But while recipes are great, especially when you're unfamiliar with a particular vegetable or technique, it's even better to have a basic technique locked down, with a few go-to bells and whistles. With that in mind, here is my basic blueprint for roasting. See page 81 for a handful of ideas for ways to upgrade virtually anything you pull from the oven (or grill, for that matter).

THE BLUEPRINT

ROASTING VEGETABLES

1. Crank up your oven. I like to roast hot, anywhere from 450°F to 500°F, so the vegetables cook quickly but have a chance to develop those beautiful caramelized edges before the rest of them is too soft.

2. Cut the vegetables into pieces that are more or less equal in size and shape, so they finish cooking at the same time. Small pieces cook more quickly but don't always have enough time to get good and brown before they're overcooked. So I tend to use pieces on the larger side—broccoli and cauliflower in big florets, fat carrots cut in half lengthwise, and green beans whole. Oh, and once you've washed those vegetables, drain and dry them well. Otherwise, you'll be sacrificing the dry heat that makes roasted vegetables so awesome.

3. Don't worry about how much you've got. There's no need to measure by weight or in cups. As long as you can spread the vegetables in a single layer on a baking sheet with a little space between each piece, you're good. Otherwise, they'll steam, not roast. If they don't fit comfortably on one baking sheet, divide the mixture between two. I like to line the baking sheet with parchment paper (not foil, which can create off-flavors) to prevent sticking and make clean-up easy.

4. Put the pieces in a bowl and drizzle on olive oil or an oil with a neutral flavor, like grapeseed or canola. Toss with your hands, rubbing the oil onto the vegetables and adding more if necessary. You want to add enough that they're well coated but not so much that pools of oil form at the bottom of the bowl. Next, add salt, tossing as you do so the vegetables get an even, generous sprinkling.

5. Spread the vegetables on a baking sheet or other large pan so that they lie flat in one layer. Roast until the bottoms are deep golden brown (start checking after 10 minutes or so), then flip or toss the vegetables so that most of that color is facing up. Keep roasting until the vegetables are as tender as you like them. I almost always flash them under the broiler after I flip them to get great color before they overcook, but doneness is a matter of preference. Taste them often: Maybe your vegetables are done when you flip them—I like a little crunch myself. If they're too firm for you, just give them a little more time in the oven.

DOUBLE UP: Buy a second baking sheet. That way, with just another minute or two of prep, you'll end up with twice what you need for dinner—and plenty of no-effort awesomeness for the days to come.

ROASTED KALE

WITH TOMATOES AND GARLIC

Kale rarely sees the inside of the oven, and that's too bad. Roasting the leafy green gives it an awesome texture somewhere between tender sautéed kale and crispy kale chips. Tomatoes add little bursts of excitement, the heat concentrating their flavor so even lackluster specimens come out jammy and sweet.

SERVES 4 TO 6
Active time: 10 MINUTES
Start to finish: 30 MINUTES

1 pound kale, such as lacinato (Tuscan), curly, or Russian, bottom inch of stems trimmed, leaves cut or torn into bite-sized pieces

2 tablespoons extra-virgin olive oil

2 garlic cloves, finely chopped

1 pint cherry tomatoes or small tomatoes cut into wedges

Kosher salt

1. Preheat the oven to 500°F. Position a rack in the upper third and another in the lower third of the oven.

2. In a large bowl, toss the kale with the oil, garlic, tomatoes, and ½ to 1 teaspoon of salt.

3. Divide the mixture between two large rimmed baking sheets and spread evenly in more or less one layer. Roast, switching the position of the pans halfway through, until the kale is tender and crisp at the edges and the tomatoes start to burst and caramelize, 15 to 20 minutes. Transfer to a serving bowl and season with more salt to taste.

CHARRED CABBAGE

WITH SPICY AÏOLI

Mild-mannered and crunchy when raw, cabbage transforms in the oven, growing sweeter by the second. I roast it in thick slices, the outer layer getting deeply brown and potato-chip crispy while the meaty core turns juicy. Spicy aïoli, aka garlicky mayo spiked with Sriracha, takes it to the next level. It's impress-your-friends stuff, though there's no shame in substituting a cup of store-bought mayo mixed with a grated clove of garlic, the juice of half a lemon, and a tablespoon or so of your favorite hot sauce.

SERVES 4 TO 6
Active time: 15 MINUTES
Start to finish: 45 MINUTES

FOR THE CABBAGE

One 2-pound head of green cabbage, bottom trimmed, outer leaves removed, sliced into ¾-inch-thick slabs

1 tablespoon extra-virgin olive oil

Kosher salt

FOR THE SPICY AÏOLI

1 large egg

4 teaspoons fresh lemon juice

1 tablespoon Sriracha, or more if you like it spicier

1 small garlic clove

Kosher salt

⅔ cup mild olive oil or grapeseed oil

1. Preheat the oven to 425°F.

2. Place the cabbage slabs on a large rimmed baking sheet and rub them with oil to coat. (Lining the pan with parchment paper is a good idea here, but up to you.) Generously season both sides of the cabbage slabs with salt. Place the cabbage cut-side down in a single layer with a little space between each one. Roast without flipping until the cabbage is tender and the bottoms are deep golden brown, 35 to 45 minutes. Flip the slices and roast for 5 minutes. Transfer the cabbage to a serving platter and season with salt to taste.

3. While the cabbage roasts, make the aïoli: Combine the egg, lemon juice, Sriracha, garlic, and ½ teaspoon salt in a blender. Start blending, then with the motor running, pour in the oil in a thin, steady stream until you've added it all. Keep blending until the aïoli is thick and creamy. Season to taste with more salt if necessary.

4. Slather some aïoli on the cabbage, reserving any extra for another use.

ROASTED BROCCOLI

WITH LEMON, CAPERS, AND SHAVED PARMESAN

The jury's still out on steamed broccoli, but roast it and everyone's on board. High, dry heat makes it extra sweet and adds an extra dimension of texture: The florets get tender but stay snappy, and the buds turn brown and crispy. Salty capers and shaved Parmesan make each bite even better. To up your game, add the lemons to the bowl with the broccoli and oil and roast the citrus cut side down, directly on the baking sheet. That way, their tartness becomes way less harsh and much more interesting. Don't sleep on broccoli's thick stalks—they're super sweet and juicy when cooked. Just peel the woody outsides.

SERVES 4 TO 6
Active time: 10 MINUTES
Start to finish: 30 MINUTES

2 heads broccoli
3 tablespoons extra-virgin olive oil
Kosher salt
1 to 2 lemons, halved
2 tablespoons capers in brine, drained
A chunk of Parmesan
Freshly ground black pepper

1. Set two large rimmed baking sheets in the upper third of the oven and preheat the oven to 500°F.

2. Cut the broccoli into large florets. Use a vegetable peeler to remove the outer layer from the large stalks—you may see their tough white fibers as you whittle them down; keep peeling until they're gone. If they're really thick, halve them lengthwise; otherwise, leave them whole.

3. In a large bowl, combine the broccoli, oil, and ½ to ¾ teaspoon salt and toss well. Spread the vegetables evenly in more or less one layer on the baking sheets, placing the lemons cut-side down directly on the pan. Roast without stirring until the stems are tender but still slightly crunchy and the edges and buds are golden brown, about 20 minutes.

4. Remove the sheets from the oven and use tongs to squeeze the lemons over the broccoli. Transfer to a serving bowl and toss with the capers; then use a vegetable peeler to shave on about ½ cup Parmesan. Season with salt and pepper to taste.

ROASTED GREEN BEANS

WITH SHALLOTS AND PARSLEY

Roast green beans once and you'll never go back to boiling them. A hot oven does its thing, leaving them wrinkled and charred with a meaty bite. Shallots amp up the flavor, a little butter adds just enough richness, and a last-minute flurry of parsley provides a blast of freshness. For a Chinese-ish variation, try swapping the salt for a few splashes of soy sauce, the butter for a little drizzle of toasted sesame oil, and the parsley for a dab of chile paste.

SERVES 4 TO 6
Active time: 10 MINUTES
Start to finish: 25 MINUTES

1½ pounds green beans, trimmed

2 tablespoons grapeseed or vegetable oil

1 large shallot, thinly sliced

Kosher salt

1 tablespoon unsalted butter

Handful of roughly chopped fresh parsley

1 lemon, halved

1. Put two large baking sheets on a rack in the upper third of the oven and preheat the oven to 500°F.

2. In a large bowl, toss the green beans with the oil, shallot, and a few generous pinches of salt. Carefully spread the vegetables evenly in more or less one layer on the hot baking sheets and turn the broiler to high. Cook, shaking the baking sheets once, until the beans are tender, wrinkled, and charred, about 10 minutes.

3. Remove the baking sheets from the oven, add the butter, and stir as it melts. Scrape it all into a serving bowl, add the parsley, and toss well. Season with lemon juice and more salt to taste.

ROASTED ROOTS AND SPICES

A classic root vegetable roast with a twist, this one's ignited by a blend of whole toasted spices that crackle between your teeth and unleash big flavor. The mix of roots includes kohlrabi, an oddball bulb that causes double takes at the farmer's market—what is *that?*—but has an irresistible sweet, cabbage-y flavor that'll win you over at first bite. Of course, virtually any combo of roots and tubers, or just one variety, works here, so feel free to swap in parsnips, celery root, rutabaga, radishes, and sweet potato.

SERVES 4 TO 6
Active time: 15 MINUTES
Start to finish: 45 MINUTES

5 large carrots, peeled and cut into 1-inch pieces

2 medium purple top turnips, peeled and cut into 1-inch pieces

2 medium kohlrabi, peeled and cut into 1-inch pieces

1 medium yellow onion, cut into 1-inch wedges

2 tablespoons extra-virgin olive oil

2 teaspoons coriander seeds

1 teaspoon caraway seeds

1 teaspoon cumin seeds

Kosher salt

2 tablespoons unsalted butter

2 tablespoons sherry or red wine vinegar, or to taste

1. Set a rimmed baking sheet on the highest rack and preheat the oven to 450°F.

2. Combine the carrots, turnips, kohlrabi, and onion in a bowl. Add the olive oil, coriander, caraway, cumin, and ½ to 1 teaspoon salt and toss well. Spread the mixture in a single layer on the preheated baking sheet. Roast until the vegetables are tender and browned in places, about 30 minutes.

3. Remove the baking sheet from the oven, add the butter, and stir to coat the vegetables as it melts. Transfer the vegetables to a serving bowl and toss with the vinegar and salt to taste.

BALSAMIC ROASTED EGGPLANT

WITH BASIL

Eggplant is usually cooked and *then* marinated, but I do the opposite. A ten-minute dunk in a bath of balsamic and olive oil lets the flavor soak in. Then into the oven it goes, the heat caramelizing the sugars in the balsamic, so it tastes even more complex and awesome. If I want to brighten the flavor, I'll drizzle on a little more balsamic just before serving.

SERVES 4 TO 6
Active time: **10 MINUTES**
Start to finish: **45 MINUTES**

2 pounds eggplant, tops trimmed, cut into 1-inch pieces

⅓ cup extra-virgin olive oil

¼ cup balsamic vinegar

Kosher salt

Big handful of fresh basil leaves, torn at the last minute

1. Preheat the oven to 500°F.

2. Put the eggplant in a large bowl, drizzle on the oil and balsamic, and sprinkle with ¾ to 1¼ teaspoons salt. Toss to coat the eggplant well and let marinate for 10 minutes.

3. Divide the eggplant between two large rimmed baking sheets and spread it evenly in more or less one layer. Roast, switching the position of the pans halfway through, until the eggplant is golden brown and creamy inside, 30 to 35 minutes. Transfer to a serving bowl, scatter on the basil, and season with more salt to taste.

CHILE-ROASTED CORN

WITH SCALLIONS AND LIME

It's hard to think of a more compelling trio than these summer treats. Because corn isn't quite a vegetable—technically it's a grain—I go big on scallions, roasting a ton of them whole with the corn so they turn super sweet.

SERVES 4 TO 6
Active time: 10 MINUTES
Start to finish: 35 MINUTES

3 large jalapeño or 2 small poblano chiles

3 cups corn kernels (from 3 or 4 large ears); see opposite

2 bunches of scallions, roots trimmed, cut into 2-inch pieces

2 tablespoons extra-virgin olive oil

Kosher salt

2 tablespoons unsalted butter

Handful of coarsely chopped fresh cilantro

1 tablespoon fresh lime juice

1. Preheat the broiler and position an oven rack 6 inches from the heat.

2. If using jalapeños, halve them lengthwise, removing the seeds and veins if you want the dish less spicy, then cut them into ¼-inch slices. If using poblanos, remove the seeds and veins and cut the chiles into ½-inch-wide strips.

3. In a large bowl, combine the chiles, corn, scallions, oil, and ½ to 1 teaspoon salt and toss well. Spread the mixture evenly in more or less one layer on a large rimmed baking sheet. Broil, tossing once or twice, until the scallions are tender and lightly charred in spots and the corn is charred but still has bite, about 10 minutes.

4. Remove it from the oven, add the butter, and stir to coat the vegetables as it melts. Scrape everything into a serving bowl, add the cilantro, lime juice, and salt to taste and toss well.

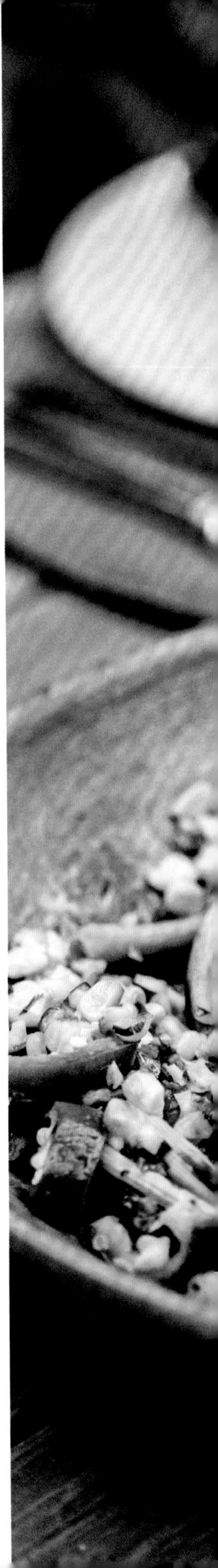

CUTTING CORN KERNELS FROM THE COB: Shuck the corn and snap or trim off any stalk remaining at the base. Stand the corn on its base in the center of a large baking dish and steady it with one hand. With the other, use a sharp chef's knife to remove the kernels, starting an inch or so from the tip of the cob and cutting down, as close to the cob as you can. The closer you cut to the cob, the less likely the kernels are to scatter. Just take care not to knock the knife against the rim of the baking dish, which could damage your blade.

GRILL THOSE VEGETABLES

IF PEOPLE GRILL vegetables at all, they tend to be an afterthought. Think of that carefully charred steak, which you can barely wait to eat, next to sad zucchini or bland, watery peppers, which you quietly push aside. Well, let those days be over.

To me, there's no better way to get big flavor out of vegetables than throwing them on scalding grates over a hot fire. With a little care, you can harness the same smoky goodness that makes grilled meat so awesome to turn vegetables into the stars of the meal.

Sometimes, that means reinvigorating old standards: Instead of grilling thin strips of zucchini, which turn mushy by the time they pick up color, I go for big honking halves that have time to develop deep, dark brown patches before they lose their snap.

Sometimes, that means welcoming new friends to the party, using the grill's intense heat to elevate broccoli, cauliflower, Swiss chard, and other vegetables rarely cooked outdoors. And whatever you grill deserves some love once it comes off those grates, so these recipes apply the chef-tested formula for making all things taste better—that exhilarating combination of a little fat, salt, and acid that makes you eager for the next bite.

All in all, the dishes in this chapter apply a few simple principles guaranteed to raise your grill game. But whether or not you choose to follow any of these recipes, the principles described here give you the tools to make vegetables the first thing on your plate you'll want to eat. And when vegetables taste this good, you'll happily eat more of them. And when you eat more of them, you're eating better.

THE BLUEPRINT

GRILLING VEGETABLES

1. Crank up the heat really high. Most of my favorite vegetables to grill are those you could eat raw, so you really don't have to worry about undercooking them. And high heat lets stuff like asparagus, zucchini, fennel, and cauliflower get plenty of flavor-boosting char before it's overcooked. If you're using gas, just turn the knob and preheat the grates. If you're using charcoal (which gives you even better flavor), light a pile of coals that comes a few inches shy of the grates and let the flames die down, just like you'd do for meat. When the coals turn a glowing gray, you're ready to cook.

2. Cut the vegetables into big pieces that are more or less equal in size. Big because that makes them easier to manage on the grill—they won't fall through the grates—and because they'll have a chance to char before they get mushy. (The bigger they are, the more contrast you'll have between the charred exterior and crisp, raw interior, so you can adjust the size to your liking.) You want the pieces similar in size so they all finish cooking at around the same time.

3. Put the pieces in a bowl and drizzle on a neutral-flavored oil, like grapeseed or vegetable oil. (Olive oil can burn over very high heat.) Toss with your hands, rubbing the oil onto the vegetables to coat them in a thin layer, then add salt as you toss so the vegetables get an even, generous sprinkling. Pour a little oil on a rag, grab the rag with tongs, and rub the oil onto the grill grates, which helps keep food from sticking.

4. Grill, turning over the pieces as they begin to char and keeping an eye out for hot spots—places on the grill where the vegetables get darker more quickly. Shuffle the vegetables if necessary so nothing gets burnt. Cook until you like what you see; I tend to think the more color the better. Consider dressing the result up a bit (see page 81), or eat them as is.

CHARRED BROCCOLI

WITH LIME, FISH SAUCE, BASIL, AND PEANUTS

If you like roasted broccoli, you're going to love it grilled. I like to keep the florets big; they're not only easy to handle but they also have time to develop crispy buds and deep, dark char before the stems lose their snap. Broccoli's nooks and crannies make it a great vehicle for dressing, like this Thai-style concoction—salty from umami-packed fish sauce, tart from lime juice, and sweet from just enough brown sugar (brown because of its flavor, not because it's any healthier than white). A final sprinkling of roasted peanuts and fresh basil completes the dish's trip to addictive territory. Add a teaspoon or so of minced fresh chile to the dressing, if heat's your thing.

SERVES 4 TO 6
Active time: **15 MINUTES**
Start to finish: **45 MINUTES**

2 tablespoons vegetable oil, plus more for the grill
¼ cup fish sauce
2 tablespoons brown sugar (light or dark)
3 tablespoons fresh lime juice
2 large heads of broccoli, bottom ½ inch trimmed, stalks peeled
Kosher salt
¼ cup coarsely chopped unsalted roasted peanuts
Handful of fresh basil leaves, torn at the last minute

1. Preheat a gas or charcoal grill to high heat. Pour a little oil on a rag, grab the rag with tongs, and rub the oil onto the grill grates to prevent sticking.

2. Whisk together the fish sauce, brown sugar, and lime juice to taste in a small bowl until the sugar dissolves.

3. Cut the broccoli into florets about 4 inches long, with plenty of stalk. Combine the broccoli, oil, and a generous sprinkle of salt in a large bowl and toss well.

4. Grill the broccoli over direct heat, flipping occasionally, until the stalks are crisp-tender and blackened in places and the buds are slightly crunchy, 8 to 12 minutes total. Transfer to a serving platter.

5. Drizzle the dressing over the broccoli and sprinkle on the peanuts and basil. Season with salt to taste.

CHARRED ZUCCHINI

WITH YOGURT, CHILES, MINT, AND LIME

For a lot of home cooks, their first time grilling zucchini is their last—just when you start to see the golden-brown color you're after, the typical thin strips have already turned mushy. Instead, do what I do: Char monster pieces over high heat and pull them while they've still got a bit of crunch. Then hit them with something rich but still fresh tasting, in this case yogurt sparked with lime juice, mint, and fresh chiles.

SERVES 4 TO 6
Active time: 15 MINUTES
Start to finish: 20 MINUTES

- 3 tablespoons grapeseed or vegetable oil, plus more for the grill
- 1 or 2 limes, to taste
- ½ cup Greek-style yogurt
- Kosher salt and black pepper
- 4 medium zucchini, halved lengthwise
- 1 hot red chile, such as Thai bird or red serrano, seeded and sliced, or to taste
- Handful of fresh mint leaves

1. Preheat a gas or charcoal grill to high heat. Pour a little oil on a rag, grab the rag with tongs, and rub the oil onto the grill grates to prevent sticking.

2. Starting with 1 lime, finely grate the zest into the yogurt, squeeze in the juice, add a few generous pinches of salt and pepper, and stir well. Taste and add more lime zest and juice to taste. Gradually add water, if needed, just until the mixture is drizzle-able (2 to 3 tablespoons should do it).

3. Rub the zucchini with the oil and season generously with salt. Grill the zucchini over direct heat, turning occasionally, until charred in places and tender but still slightly crunchy, 5 to 8 minutes total. Transfer to a serving platter.

4. Serve the yogurt sauce with the zucchini and then sprinkle with the chile and plenty of mint.

GRILLED CAULIFLOWER STEAKS

WITH GRAPEFRUIT, WATERCRESS, AND PECANS

Cauliflower heads carved into thick slabs are substantial enough to eat with a fork and knife, and they pick up smoky, seared flavor when grilled. Here, I top those golden-brown steaks with sweet-tart citrus, peppery watercress, and rich pecans. They're not a rib eye, but they *are* really good.

SERVES 4
Active time: 25 MINUTES
Start to finish: 45 MINUTES

¼ cup grapeseed or vegetable oil, plus more for the grill

2 small heads of cauliflower, bottoms trimmed flat

Kosher salt

2 large grapefruit

1 tablespoon white balsamic or white wine vinegar

1 large bunch (6 ounces) of watercress or arugula, thick stems trimmed

½ cup pecans, toasted, crumbled if large

1. Preheat a gas or charcoal grill to high heat. Pour a little oil on a rag, grab the rag with tongs, and rub the oil onto the grill grates to prevent sticking.

2. One by one, stand each cauliflower head, florets up, on a cutting board and cut the cauliflower into thirds, making sure each piece includes some of the stem so the pieces hold together. Rub the pieces on both sides with 2 tablespoons of the oil and season generously with salt.

3. Grill over direct heat, flipping once, until crisp-tender and charred on both sides, 6 to 8 minutes per side. Transfer to a serving platter.

4. Meanwhile, trim the tops and bottoms of the grapefruit with a sharp knife. Working from top to bottom and following the curve of the fruit, carve off the peel and pith to expose the flesh. Working over a bowl, cut each grapefruit segment from the membrane and drop it in the bowl. When you're done, squeeze any juice from the membranes into the bowl, then discard the membranes. Pour the juices into a small bowl, whisk together with the remaining 2 tablespoons oil, and season with salt to taste to make the dressing.

5. In a big bowl, gently toss the watercress with some of the grapefruit dressing. Drizzle the rest of grapefruit dressing onto the cauliflower steaks, sprinkle with the pecans, then top with the grapefruit segments and watercress.

GRILLED RADICCHIO

WITH SHERRY-HONEY VINAIGRETTE AND HAZELNUTS

I love everything about radicchio—the striking burgundy color, the intense flavor, and the sturdy leaves, which stand up so well to heat. A quick turn on the grill mellows its bitterness (a touch of honey in the dressing helps, too) and mixes up the texture, giving you crisp singed edges and tender inner leaves. With vinegar delivering complex acidity and hazelnuts (or almonds, if you've got them) providing crunch and good fat, you'll have a happy crowd at your table.

SERVES 4 TO 6
Active time: 15 MINUTES
Start to finish: 30 MINUTES

1 tablespoon grapeseed or vegetable oil, plus more for the grill

3 medium heads of radicchio

Kosher salt

2 tablespoons sherry or red wine vinegar

1 tablespoon honey

2 tablespoons extra-virgin olive oil

¼ cup chopped unsalted roasted hazelnuts or almonds

1. Preheat a gas or charcoal grill to high heat. Pour a little oil on a rag, grab the rag with tongs, and rub the oil onto the grill grates to prevent sticking.

2. Quarter the radicchio through the core into wedges. Rub the wedges with the grapeseed oil and generously season with salt. Grill the radicchio over direct heat until charred in places and slightly wilted, 8 to 10 minutes. Transfer to a serving platter.

3. Combine the vinegar, honey, olive oil, and a few generous pinches of salt in a small bowl and whisk well. Drizzle the dressing over the radicchio, sprinkle on the hazelnuts, and season with salt to taste.

GRILLED SWISS CHARD

WITH FENNEL AND SAUSAGE

A while back, I was outside hanging with friends and barbecuing some pork, when I lost track of time. All the food was almost ready, but I looked down and realized I had a pile of chard I had planned to bring back inside and sauté. So I took a chance. I stacked the chard on the grill and hoped for the best. The result blew me away—the stems tender and the leaves silky with crisp, brown edges—a happy accident that inspired a go-to technique. Here, it teams up with fennel, another grill-friendly vegetable, and sausage.

SERVES 4 TO 6
Active time: 20 MINUTES
Start to finish: 35 MINUTES

4 tablespoons grapeseed or vegetable oil, plus more for the grill

4 medium fennel bulbs, outer layer removed

1 large bunch of Swiss chard, bottom 1 inch of stems trimmed

Kosher salt

1 or 2 links sweet or spicy Italian-style sausage

1 lemon, halved

A chunk of pecorino cheese

1. Preheat a gas or charcoal grill to high heat. Pour a little oil on a rag, grab the rag with tongs, and rub the oil onto the grill grates to prevent sticking.

2. Cut the fennel into ½-inch wedges through the core, put them in a large bowl, and drizzle on 2 tablespoons of the oil, and a few generous pinches of salt, tossing and rubbing to coat them well. In another bowl, do the same with the chard, salt, and the remaining 2 tablespoons of oil.

3. Grill the fennel and sausage over direct heat, flipping occasionally, until the fennel is charred and crisp-tender and the sausage is golden brown and cooked through, about 15 minutes. Make one big pile of the chard (no need for a neat stack, but you should be able to grab the whole thing with tongs) and add it to the grill over direct heat, flipping the pile occasionally, until tender, and charred at the edges, about 6 minutes. Transfer the chard and sausage to a cutting board. Transfer the fennel to a large serving bowl.

4. Coarsely chop the Swiss chard and the sausage, add them to the bowl with the fennel, squeeze on a couple tablespoons of lemon juice, and toss well. Use a vegetable peeler to shave about ½ cup of the pecorino, toss, and season with salt to taste.

CHARRED ESCAROLE AND GRILLED BREAD

WITH RICOTTA AND PINE NUTS

Escarole looks like a regular head of lettuce, but it's got so much more going for it. The sturdy leaves can stand up to the heat of the grill, retaining their slightly meaty texture as they wilt, and the green's flavor goes from bitter to exciting. Heaped on ricotta-topped, garlic-rubbed toast, there's nothing better. (The grilled escarole is also great served with fish or chicken.)

SERVES 6
Active time: 25 MINUTES
Start to finish: 35 MINUTES

2 tablespoons grapeseed or vegetable oil, plus more for the grill

2 heads of escarole

Kosher salt

6 thick slices country-style bread

¼ cup extra-virgin olive oil

1 large garlic clove, halved

1½ cups fresh ricotta cheese

1 teaspoon finely grated lemon zest

2 to 3 tablespoons fresh lemon juice

¼ cup pine nuts, toasted

1. Preheat a gas or charcoal grill to high heat. Pour a little oil on a rag, grab the rag with tongs, and rub the oil onto the grill grates to prevent sticking.

2. Halve the escarole lengthwise, rinse the halves under cold running water, and shake them over the sink so they're no longer very wet. Drizzle the grapeseed oil over the escarole, separating the leaves so the oil drips between them but keeping the heads intact. Season the escarole generously with salt.

3. Grill the escarole over direct heat, turning occasionally, until the outer leaves are charred in places and the inner leaves are tender, 6 to 10 minutes. Transfer to a cutting board.

4. While the escarole is grilling, brush both sides of the bread with the olive oil, season with salt, and grill over direct heat, turning occasionally, until charred and crunchy but still soft in the middle, about 6 minutes. Transfer to serving plates. Rub the cut end of the garlic against one side of each toast. Top with the ricotta and a pinch of salt.

5. Coarsely chop the escarole and put it in a large bowl with the lemon zest and juice to taste. Season with salt to taste, then pile the escarole on the toasts. Sprinkle the pine nuts on top.

GRILLED ASPARAGUS

WITH BUTTERED LEEKS

A grill needs barely any time to take asparagus from unassuming to charred, sweet, and juicy. High heat, a little attention—pull them while they still have plenty of bite—and maybe a squeeze of lemon are really all you need. But I stack the deck by adding buttery leeks and a vinaigrette packed with shallots and asparagus's best friend, tarragon. Oh, and these leeks are great on lots of dishes, especially with fish.

SERVES 4 TO 6
Active time: 20 MINUTES
Start to finish: 45 MINUTES

3 large leeks, dark green parts removed

1 cup low-sodium chicken stock

4 tablespoons (½ stick) unsalted butter

Kosher salt

1 large shallot, finely chopped

1½ tablespoons white wine vinegar

2 tablespoons extra-virgin olive oil

1 tablespoon chopped fresh tarragon leaves (or a handful of basil leaves, torn)

1 tablespoon grapeseed or vegetable oil, plus more for the grill

1½ pounds asparagus, trimmed (see below)

1. Thinly slice the leeks crosswise, put them in a large bowl of cold water, and agitate them a bit, so any sand and grit falls to the bottom.

2. Bring the stock and butter to a simmer over medium heat in a large heavy skillet and stir in ¼ to ½ teaspoon of salt. With a slotted spoon, scoop the leeks from the water into the skillet. Cover and cook until the leeks have wilted, about 8 minutes. Uncover the skillet and simmer until the leeks are very tender and the stock has evaporated into a glaze, about 4 minutes. Transfer the leeks to a serving platter.

3. To make the vinaigrette, combine the shallot, vinegar, and a few pinches of salt in a small bowl and let stand for 5 minutes or so. Whisk in the olive oil and stir in the tarragon.

4. Preheat a gas or charcoal grill to high heat.

5. Toss the asparagus with the grapeseed oil and generously sprinkle with salt. Grill over direct heat, rotating once or twice, until the stalks are charred but still have a snap, 5 to 7 minutes total. Put the asparagus on the leeks and drizzle with the vinaigrette.

TRIMMING ASPARAGUS: To prep asparagus, snap off the tough bottoms. While they aren't fun to chew on, they're full of flavor. Try simmering them in chicken stock until you have a broth that tastes like springtime. Use the broth for soup or Basic Farro Risotto (page 241).

LEVEL-UP YOUR VEGETABLES

After roasting or grilling nearly any vegetable, add any of these easy, interchangeable combinations of toppings to turn simple into special. Each one applies the magic formula for making food taste better: Add acid, salt, fat, or texture. The amounts I provide are loose, because you really can't go wrong.

- Dollops of Greek yogurt + big handful of pomegranate seeds + big handful of coarsely chopped fresh parsley or cilantro *(so good with roasted carrots or grilled eggplant)*
- Generous squeeze of lime + handful of toasted pumpkin seeds + generous topping of crumbled queso fresco *(so good with roasted or grilled scallions, zucchini, and radishes)*
- A tablespoon or two sherry vinegar + big handful of crumbled manchego or Parmesan + handful of toasted, coarsely chopped almonds *(so good with roasted red onions and parsnips, grilled beets, or Swiss chard)*
- Handful of toasted, coarsely chopped walnuts + a drizzle of honey + big handful of grated Parmesan and a splash of white wine vinegar *(so good with roasted or grilled radicchio and cauliflower)*
- Generous pinch of finely grated lemon zest + liberal topping of crumbled goat cheese + handful of chopped fresh chives *(so good with roasted mushrooms or grilled asparagus)*
- Generous squeeze of lime juice + a few dashes of fish sauce + big handful of chopped fresh mint, cilantro, and/or scallions *(so good with roasted Brussels sprouts and snap peas or grilled cabbage)*

AND ONE MORE TIP. CHAR YOUR LEMONS: Cut a lemon in half crosswise, flick out the seeds, and rub the cut sides with a little oil. Place the halves cut-side down on the baking sheet or grill grates along with your vegetables and cook as usual. By the time they're done, the lemon will have charred and its juice will be tart and complex, not just sour. Squeeze the juice over the vegetables and be prepared to fight your family and friends for every bite.

EAT
THOSE
VEGETABLES
RAW

WHEN YOU WORK in fancy restaurants, you do a lot to carrots. You roast, glaze, or pickle them. You sweat, puree, and strain them. You don't typically peel them and put them on a plate. But at home, that's exactly what you should do. Whenever you can, you should eat carrot sticks, cucumber spears, celery stalks, kohlrabi batons, pepper slices, cherry tomatoes, whole radishes, and handfuls of watercress. No, I'm not advocating a raw food diet. I'm just acknowledging that you'll eat more vegetables if you make the task as easy as possible. And as delicious.

So yes, roast broccoli and snap peas and cabbage. Grill cauliflower and asparagus and zucchini. But embrace the path of least resistance, too. This chapter is about celebrating vegetables in their most convenient form. First I'll share a collection of effortless dips that'll convince even expert cooks to stop dicing and start dunking. Next are my favorite salads that come together quickly and don't require cooking—except the one that requires frying up a little bacon, but my guess is that most of us don't mind doing that.

DIPS FOR CRUDITÉ

GUACAMOLE

When you mash ripe avocado with plenty of lime and salt, you've got a great dip. But the key to my guacamole is the simple, flavor-packed paste of onion, chile, and a touch of garlic. Just a minute in a mortar or food processor gives you a supercharged mix-in that ensures that each creamy chunk gets some of the good stuff.

MAKES ABOUT 1½ CUPS
Active time: 10 MINUTES
Start to finish: 10 MINUTES

¼ cup chopped white onion

1 fresh serrano or jalapeño chile (seeds removed, if you want it less spicy), finely chopped

½ small garlic clove, finely chopped

Kosher salt

3 ripe Hass avocados

1 or 2 limes, halved

⅓ cup crumbled queso fresco (optional)

¼ cup coarsely chopped fresh cilantro

1. Mash the onion, chile, garlic, and ½ to ¾ teaspoon salt to a pretty fine paste in a mortar and pestle (or a Mexican molcajete). You can also pulse them in a small food processor, or just chop them together, finely, by hand. Transfer the mixture to a large bowl.

2. Halve the avocados, pry out the pits, and scoop the flesh into the bowl with the chile mixture. Coarsely mash the avocado and stir it in. Squeeze in lots of lime juice while tasting the guacamole—when you think you've added just enough, add a little more. Stir gently and add more salt to taste. Sprinkle with the queso fresco, if using, and cilantro.

PECAN ROMESCO
HERBAGANOUSH
CHIPOTLE-LIME AÏOLI
WHITE BEAN HUMMUS
GUACAMOLE

CHIPOTLE-LIME AÏOLI

Aïoli is a traditional dip for crudités in the South of France, but here, I take it south of the border. For this Mexican makeover, lime juice stands in for the usual lemon, and chipotle chiles in adobo, one of the tastiest canned products in existence, contribute smoky flavor and heat to the creamy, velvety condiment. To achieve a truly awesome texture, make sure to add the oil really slowly—seriously, go drop by drop at first and then pour it in a very thin stream—while blending. If you're not up for all that, just whisk the mashed garlic, lime juice, and chipotle in adobo into ½ cup store-bought mayonnaise and season with salt to taste.

MAKES ABOUT 1 CUP
Active time: 10 MINUTES
Start to finish: 10 MINUTES

4 garlic cloves, finely chopped
Kosher salt
2 large egg yolks
2 tablespoons fresh lime juice
1 teaspoon Dijon mustard
½ cup extra-virgin olive oil
6 tablespoons vegetable oil
2 tablespoons finely chopped canned chipotle in adobo

1. Use the flat side of a chef's knife to mash and scrape the garlic and big pinch of salt to a paste. Scrape the paste into a blender, food processor, or a cup for a hand blender. Add the egg yolks, lime juice, and mustard.

2. In a container with a spout, combine the olive and vegetable oils. Begin blending. Very gradually, a drop at a time at first, then in a thin, steady stream, add the oil into the egg yolk mixture. Blend until all the oil is incorporated and the mixture is thick and creamy. Blend in the chipotle in adobo and 1 tablespoon water, and season with salt to taste.

The aïoli keeps in an airtight container in the fridge for up to 3 days.

WHITE BEAN HUMMUS

For this mash-up of two great dips, I borrow the tahini, cumin, and lemon juice that grace my favorite renditions of the Middle Eastern chickpea puree, and white beans, olive oil, and parsley from the kind of dunk-worthy stuff a Tuscan cook might whip up. Canned white beans turn out even creamier than chickpeas, so this is especially awesome with anything from snap peas to radishes, cucumber to carrots, and pita to Italian breadsticks.

MAKES ABOUT 4 CUPS
Active time: **10 MINUTES**
Start to finish: **10 MINUTES**

2 garlic cloves

Two 15-ounce cans low-sodium white beans, rinsed and drained

¼ cup well-stirred tahini

¼ cup extra-virgin olive oil

1 teaspoon ground cumin

3 tablespoons fresh lemon juice

Kosher salt

½ cup chopped fresh parsley (optional)

With the motor running, drop the garlic into a food processor and process until finely chopped. Add the white beans, tahini, oil, cumin, lemon juice, and ½ teaspoon of salt. Pulse until the hummus is smooth. Season with salt to taste and stir in the parsley. if using.

The hummus keeps in an airtight container in the fridge for up to 5 days.

PECAN ROMESCO

In the Spanish region of Catalonia, the locals gather around piles of spring onions called *calçots* that have been blackened over fire and piled on newspaper. They strip off the layer of char and dangle the onions over their heads before gobbling them, just like kids do with strands of spaghetti. Yet the ritual isn't complete without dunking those tender bulbs in a fire-red sauce so good it threatens to upstage even this special vegetable. This is romesco, a coarse puree of charred tomatoes and peppers thickened with toasted bread and nuts (I use ultrarich pecans instead of the traditional almonds) and electrified by the acidity of sherry vinegar and the heat and smokiness of Spanish paprika.

Unsurprisingly, romesco is just as good with raw vegetables like bell peppers and carrots as it is with grilled ones like scallions and asparagus.

MAKES ABOUT 2 CUPS
Active time: 20 MINUTES
Start to finish: 30 MINUTES

2 large red bell peppers
1 large tomato
½ cup pecans
1 thick slice country-style bread, cut into about 1-inch pieces
3 tablespoons sherry vinegar
1 large garlic clove
¾ teaspoon smoked paprika
Kosher salt
⅓ cup extra-virgin olive oil

1. Preheat the oven to 400°F.

2. Turn a gas flame to medium high and set the peppers and tomato on the grates over the flame. (If your stove is electric, broil the peppers and tomato on a baking sheet on the rack closest to the heat.) Cook, turning occasionally, until the skins are blistered and blackened all over, 8 to 10 minutes. Transfer the peppers and tomato to a bowl, cover tightly with plastic wrap, and let them stand and steam until cool enough to handle, about 15 minutes. Peel the skins off the peppers and tomato and remove the stems and seeds from the pepper. Coarsely chop the vegetables and transfer to a blender or food processor.

3. While the vegetables are steaming, spread the nuts and bread in a single layer on a baking sheet and bake until the bread turns golden and slightly crunchy, about 8 minutes. Transfer the nuts and bread to the blender with the peppers and tomato. Add the vinegar, garlic, paprika, and ½ to 1 teaspoon salt and blend until pretty smooth. With the motor running, pour in the oil and blend until very smooth. Season with more salt to taste.

The romesco keeps in an airtight container in the fridge for up to 5 days.

HERBAGANOUSH

My favorite part of this eggplant dip isn't listed as an ingredient. It comes from the cooking method: When you char eggplant directly on hot coals (or on a baking sheet under the broiler), the flesh takes on an irresistible smoky flavor even after you peel away the blackened skins. I skip the garlic and tahini that goes into most baba ganoush and load mine with herbs for a lighter, fresher, aromatic dip. It's a great way to add color and flavor, and to use up any herbs you have knocking around in the fridge.

MAKES ABOUT 2 CUPS
Active time: 10 MINUTES
Start to finish: 35 MINUTES

1 large eggplant

Big handful of coarsely chopped mixed fresh herbs, such as parsley, marjoram, oregano, basil, and chives

2 tablespoons fresh lemon juice

¼ cup extra-virgin olive oil

Kosher salt

1. Preheat a grill, preferably with hardwood charcoal. When the coals stop flaming and turn gray, spread them out and put the eggplant directly on the coals. (You can approximate this with a gas grill by using high heat and putting the eggplant on the grates, or broil it on a baking sheet as close as possible to the heating element.) Cook, turning occasionally, until the skin is completely charred and the eggplant is very tender all the way to the center, 20 to 25 minutes. Transfer the eggplant to a large plate and let it hang out until it's cool enough to handle.

2. Peel back and discard the charred skin and scrape the flesh into a food processor. Add the herbs, lemon juice, olive oil, and ½ to 1 teaspoon of salt. Pulse until you have a pretty chunky puree. Season with more salt to taste.

The herbaganoush keeps in an airtight container in the fridge for up to 5 days.

RED SLAW WITH WARM BACON DRESSING

Yep, eating better can mean eating bacon. Especially when you use it as a gateway to good stuff like cabbage and peppers. Here, the salty, porky product contributes its powers of persuasion—both in crispy fried bits and as flavorful fat—to a two-ingredient dressing. Drizzled on warm, it just barely softens the sturdy vegetables, coaxing out their sweetness while keeping their crunch. This dressing is also great on sturdy raw greens and lettuces (such as spinach, radicchio, and frisée) or simply roasted vegetables like green beans, snap peas, broccoli, cauliflower, and cabbage.

SERVES 4 TO 6
Active time: 10 MINUTES
Start to finish: 20 MINUTES

1 small head of red cabbage, bruised outer leaves removed, very thinly sliced

1 medium red bell pepper, stemmed, seeded, and cut into long, thin strips

6 ounces bacon slices, cut into about ½-inch pieces

¼ cup plus 2 tablespoons sherry or apple cider vinegar

Kosher salt

1. Combine the cabbage and pepper in a large bowl. If they're cold, let them come to room temperature.

2. Put the bacon in a large heavy skillet, set it over medium heat, and cook, stirring occasionally, until it releases its fat and turns brown and crisp, 8 to 10 minutes. Remove the skillet from the heat and stir in the vinegar and ¼ to ½ teaspoon salt.

3. While it's still warm, pour the dressing over the cabbage and pepper and toss well. Season with more salt to taste.

SHAVED ZUCCHINI SALAD

Raw zucchini might not sound exciting, but slicing it into thin ribbons—either on a mandoline or with a vegetable peeler—shows off its delicate crunch and subtle sweetness. I especially like treating zucchini this way in the summer when it grows like crazy and I don't feel like turning on the oven. Lemony dressing, salty curls of Parm, and fresh basil complete the very pretty picture.

SERVES 4 TO 6
Active time: 15 MINUTES
Start to finish: 15 MINUTES

2 pounds zucchini

1 teaspoon finely grated lemon zest

1½ tablespoons fresh lemon juice

3 tablespoons extra-virgin olive oil

Kosher salt and freshly ground black pepper

Big handful of thinly shaved Parmesan

Handful of fresh basil leaves

1. Use a mandoline or a vegetable peeler to shave the zucchini lengthwise into long, thin ribbons.

2. In a large bowl, whisk together the lemon zest, lemon juice, olive oil, ½ to ¾ teaspoon salt, and ½ teaspoon pepper. Add the zucchini, toss really well, and transfer to a serving platter. Scatter on the Parmesan and season with more salt and pepper to taste. Tear the basil leaves if large and scatter them on top.

BRUSSELS SPROUTS CAESAR SALAD

I wish I could say I came up with the idea of swapping out the romaine in the classic Caesar, because there's a reason you now see kale and Brussels sprouts coated in creamy, bright, anchovy-spiked dressing at restaurants from Brooklyn to Boise. These vegetables deliver flavor instead of just crunch, not to mention more nutrition. I particularly like to use Brussels sprouts, thinly sliced so they grab on tight to that I-want-to-eat-this-forever dressing. Baby spinach leaves, very thinly sliced kale, or a crunchy combination of thinly sliced celery and radishes are also great to use here instead of the sprouts.

SERVES 6 TO 8
Active time: 20 MINUTES
Start to finish: 20 MINUTES

4 thick slices crusty bread
½ cup extra-virgin olive oil
1 or 2 oil-packed anchovy fillets, finely chopped
1 garlic clove, finely chopped
Kosher salt
1 large egg yolk
2 tablespoons fresh lemon juice
1 teaspoon Dijon mustard
Freshly ground black pepper
2 pounds Brussels sprouts, bottoms trimmed, halved lengthwise, very thinly sliced
Big handful of finely grated Parmesan cheese
12 vinegared white anchovy fillets, often labeled "boquerones" (optional)

1. Drizzle both sides of the bread slices with about ¼ cup of the oil, then toast in a toaster oven or 400°F oven, flipping once, until golden on both sides, 5 to 8 minutes. Cut them into 1-inch pieces.

2. Use a fork to mash the anchovy, garlic, and a pinch of salt to a paste. Scrape the paste into a large bowl. Add the egg yolk, lemon juice, mustard, and stir well. Then while whisking, add the remaining ¼ cup oil in a thin, steady stream and keep whisking until creamy. Season with salt and pepper to taste.

3. Add the Brussels sprouts to the bowl, toss with the dressing to coat well, and season with more salt to taste. Scatter the bread and cheese on top and, if you've got them, add the white anchovies.

CANNED SALAD

When friends come over at the last minute, I pop open a few cans and jars to make this back-pocket salad. What might seem like a cop-out to dried bean devotees, members of Artichoke-Turners Anonymous, and captains of the health patrol is actually a damn good dish that comes together in minutes and requires zero time at the stove. It's also an important reminder that while fresh vegetables are best, eating vegetables of any kind is important. Plus, these preserved products pass my pantry purge test with flying colors. The key to reviving them is not holding back on lemon, so squeeze on even more than you think you'll need.

SERVES 4 TO 6
Active time: **10 MINUTES**
Start to finish: **10 MINUTES**

- One 14- to 15-ounce can low-sodium white beans or black-eyed peas, rinsed and drained
- One 14-ounce jar artichoke hearts, drained and quartered
- One 14-ounce can hearts of palm, drained and cut into about ½-inch slices
- 4 ounces crumbled feta cheese
- 3 to 4 celery stalks, peeled, cut into about ½-inch pieces, plus some coarsely chopped celery leaves
- 3 tablespoons extra-virgin olive oil
- 1 tablespoon finely grated lemon zest
- 1 or 2 lemons, halved
- Kosher salt
- ¼ cup pine nuts, toasted

Combine the beans, artichoke hearts, hearts of palm, feta cheese, celery and leaves, oil, and lemon zest in a large serving bowl. Squeeze on lots of lemon juice to make the salad taste really bright, then sprinkle on about ½ teaspoon salt. Toss really well and season with more salt to taste. Sprinkle on the pine nuts.

ARUGULA-APPLE SALAD

This salad requires no flourishes. Combine peppery arugula, crisp apple slices, crunchy almonds, and put-me-on-anything Parm in a bowl, and you're good. Still, one easy embellishment doesn't hurt: Superquick pickled onions bring the salad to the next level with addictive tartness.

SERVES 4 TO 6
Active time: 10 MINUTES
Start to finish: 10 MINUTES

½ cup thinly sliced red onion
2 tablespoons apple cider vinegar
Kosher salt
1 apple
8 ounces arugula
3 tablespoons extra-virgin olive oil
Handful of chopped fresh chives
Big handful of finely grated Parmesan
½ cup sliced almonds, toasted

1. Combine the onion, vinegar, and ½ to ¾ teaspoon salt in a large bowl. Mix well and let sit for 5 minutes or so.

2. Core and thinly slice the apple and add it to the bowl along with the arugula, oil, and chives. Toss gently but well to coat with the dressing, then sprinkle with the cheese and almond slices. Season with more salt to taste.

ALEX'S BUTTER LETTUCE SALAD

In my home, I do most of the cooking. Yet my wife, Alex, still schools me often. She whips up a tangy, creamy dressing made from buttermilk and mayo—yes, I'm down with mayo in my salad—and tosses in sweet, tender leaves of butter lettuce and crunchy radishes. It's simple. It's insanely good. I just wish I'd come up with it.

SERVES 4 TO 6
Active time: 10 MINUTES
Start to finish: 10 MINUTES

½ cup well-shaken buttermilk
2 tablespoons mayo
1 tablespoon fresh lemon juice
2 scallions, roots trimmed, very thinly sliced
Kosher salt and freshly ground black pepper
2 large heads butter lettuce, such as Bibb or Boston
6 or so small radishes, thinly sliced

1. Combine the buttermilk, mayo, lemon juice, scallions, ½ teaspoon salt, and ½ teaspoon pepper in a medium bowl and whisk until smooth.

2. Tear the lettuce heads into big leaves and put them on a serving platter, scatter on the radishes, and dress with ½ cup of the dressing or more if you like. Season with salt and pepper to taste.

CELERY-RADISH SALAD

WITH CHILES AND LIME

These two vegetables are usually cast as supporting characters, but in this salad, they're the stars of the show. They offer two types of awesome crunch, plus the kind of bold flavor—celery with its snap and radish with its peppery zing—that wakes up your palate. Lime juice and fiery fresh chiles (serranos if you can find them, jalapeños if you can't) keep the excitement level high. Salty Mexican cheese cools things down, but just barely.

SERVES 4 TO 6
Active time: 10 MINUTES
Start to finish: 10 MINUTES

1 head of celery, bottom 2 inches trimmed

6 to 8 small radishes

1 to 2 serrano or jalapeño chiles, seeds and white veins removed if you want less heat

3 tablespoons extra-virgin olive oil

1½ tablespoons fresh lime juice

Big handful of crumbled cotija cheese or queso fresco (or coarsely grated Parmesan)

Kosher salt

Thinly slice the celery crosswise, including any leaves, and put it in a large bowl. Thinly slice the radishes and chiles using a sharp knife (or a mandoline, which is even easier), add them to the bowl with the celery, and toss together with the oil, lime juice, and cheese. Season generously with salt and more lime juice to taste and serve.

MUSTARD GREEN SALAD

WITH PECANS AND HONEY-LEMON DRESSING

When the First Lady and I planted a kitchen garden on the South Lawn of the White House, the fennel, eggplant, and broccoli might have been symbolic of our quest to help Americans eat better, but they weren't ornamental. They ended up on fine china when the president hosted meals for heads of state and in bowls when the family ate together each night. They both fueled my cooking adventures and inspired them. This salad, for instance, came to be after the garden gave us way more purple mustard greens that we knew what to do with. After a little experimenting, I settled on a honey-spiked dressing that takes the edge off the greens' thrilling, sharp bite, plus croutons and pecans for crunch. I swear the First Lady and I polished off a whole bowl of it by ourselves.

SERVES 4 TO 6
Active time: 10 MINUTES
Start to finish: 20 MINUTES

3 thick slices crusty whole-wheat bread, cut into 1-inch pieces

¼ cup plus 2 tablespoons extra-virgin olive oil

Kosher salt

2 medium bunches of mild mustard greens (purple mustards are best)

1 small shallot, finely chopped

2 tablespoons fresh lemon juice

1 tablespoon honey

½ cup pecan halves, toasted

1. Preheat the oven to 400°F.

2. Spread the bread pieces on a large baking sheet, drizzle with 2 tablespoons of the oil, and toss well. Add a generous sprinkle of salt and bake, tossing once, until golden and crunchy, 10 to 12 minutes. Let cool to room temperature.

3. Meanwhile, trim the bottom 1 inch from the mustard green stems, stack the greens, tightly roll them into a cylinder, and slice them across the stems into thin ribbons. You'll have about 8 cups.

4. Combine the remaining ¼ cup oil with the shallot, lemon juice, honey, and ¼ to ½ teaspoon salt in a large bowl and whisk well. Add the mustard greens, toss well, and season with more salt to taste. Top with the croutons and pecans.

ORANGE IS THE NEW WHITE

IN THE QUEST TO EAT BETTER,

some choices are complicated. For instance, while we were once warned to avoid fats, it turns out that some fats are actually food for us. In theory, we should all choose pasta made from whole grains, but it's a hard sell since very few companies have figured out how to make it delicious. There are debates to be had, balances to be struck, and progress to be made.

Then there are choices that shouldn't be complicated at all, like that between the ubiquitous white potato and the far superior sweet potato. On average, we each eat a little more than seven pounds of sweet potatoes a year, and more than *fifty* pounds of white potatoes, about half in the form of fries and chips. We'd be much better off if it were the other way around.

But before I sing the praises of the sweet potato, I want to tell you a story about how ditching the typical tuber can have implications beyond the health of you and your family. I want to introduce you to the potato lobby.

Before I joined the Obama administration, I didn't know there was such a thing. But once I waded into the bog of food policy, I learned that practically every food—from almonds to avocados, candy to pizza—has a lobby. Despite their reputation, lobbies aren't necessarily bad. They're merely organizations that advocate for a cause or, in the case of food lobbies, an industry. The question is, is that product being pushed at the expense of people's health? In the case of the potato lobby (as well as of numerous other lobbies), the answer is a resounding yes.

Early on, we set out to improve the lunches served to kids in public schools throughout the country. By the time we had finished our push, we had passed legislation that increased the amount of vegetables, fruits, and whole grains in school lunches and reduced the amount of sodium and saturated fat—a big win for children's health.

Yet while we'd won a major battle, there was one scuffle that left me seething. The last thing we wanted was to become cynical, but the potato lobby tested our resolve. As a small part of our overall effort, in the new guidelines we decided to include a twice-a-week limit on serving French fries for lunch in schools—and those fries could no longer count as a vegetable. (It might surprise you to learn that fried potato consumption beats out even soda as an indicator of obesity.) For us, this was common sense: Parents don't give their kids fries thinking they're a substitute for nutritious vegetables, so why should the government? But the gang of well-funded groups hired to scrap for the spud treated it like a declaration of war.

Now, I'm not here to bash potatoes. Mashed, baked, roasted, they taste great. And it's not that white potatoes are *bad*, though despite the lobby's propaganda, they have only modest nutritional value. The problem is simply that we're eating way too many of them, at the expense of more nutrient-dense vegetables.

Well, the potato pushers flipped out. They did what lobbyists do: They fought viciously for the people whose interests they're paid to promote. My colleagues and I at the White House endured a series of typical hyperbolic arguments—Jobs will disappear! Farms will fold!—that tellingly had nothing to do with the well-being of kids. Yet we knew we faced a formidable adversary. Part of the lobbyists' power comes from the money they wield—because we eat so many potatoes, big growers have a lot at stake and pay a lot to protect it. And part of their power comes from the fact that ten states are major potato producers. That means the lobby has leverage over enough people in Congress (twenty senators and dozens of representatives who reliably do their bidding) to make or break legislation. Those paid to push grapefruit, avocados, and other produce grown primarily in a couple of states have no such sway.

Both sides of the battle understood that victory was about even more than the potatoes consumed by those 31 million school kids. For us, it would also mean a win for the increasingly quaint notion that science, not politics or the influence that money can buy, should drive policy—a triumph for all Americans. And because how we eat as kids determines how we'll eat as adults, victory would affect what these kids eat for the rest of their lives and what they'll ultimately feed their children. That's why the battle over children's plates is so important, and why we wanted to shift the balance ever so slightly toward nutrient-dense foods like broccoli, cauliflower, and green beans.

I'd like to tell you that our arguments prevailed, that members of Congress joined hands and declared in unison that the health of our country's children would always come before profit. No such luck. Congress gave in to Big Potato. Today, lunchrooms can serve French fries every day. The best we could do was require that an additional serving of actual vegetables accompany those fries. The potato lobby won, just like the pizza lobby—otherwise known as the Frozen Food Institute—when it convinced Congress that the tomato sauce in a cheese-covered disk of dough should count as a serving of vegetables, just as ketchup counted as a vegetable back in the 1980s.

Yet there's good news: The fight continues. Until the day when voters overwhelm their representatives and senators with phone calls before big food policy votes—which, to be sure, is a day we need to work toward—each of us can take a stand against the potato lobby by making a different choice. I can tell you that white potato consumption saw a dramatic decline on the president's own table, and I'll be damned if this book includes a single recipe for them. Instead, I'm giving some well-deserved love to sweet potatoes. They taste better. They're better for you. And eating them doesn't empower a lobby that undermines the well-being of children.

And so this chapter celebrates this almost-too-good-to-be-true vegetable, which has more fiber and vitamins and, almost magically, fewer calories despite all that awesome sweetness. Here, you'll find three categories of recipes. The first offers ways to dress up roasted sweet potatoes, which for the record taste damn good by themselves but even better with some salt, fat, and acid. The next set of recipes flaunts the luxurious texture of the roasted flesh and provide ways to set off its irresistible sweetness. The third category includes a technique for the impatient or habitually late among us who need a way to get dinner on the table in less than half the time it takes to oven-roast. Of course, my recipes represent just a few of the endless great ideas for serving sweet potatoes. The basic method—cook potato, add other good stuff—is just a jumping-off point. Experiment, riff, have fun. With sweet potatoes, it's hard to go wrong.

LOTS OF POTATOES, LOTS OF POWER

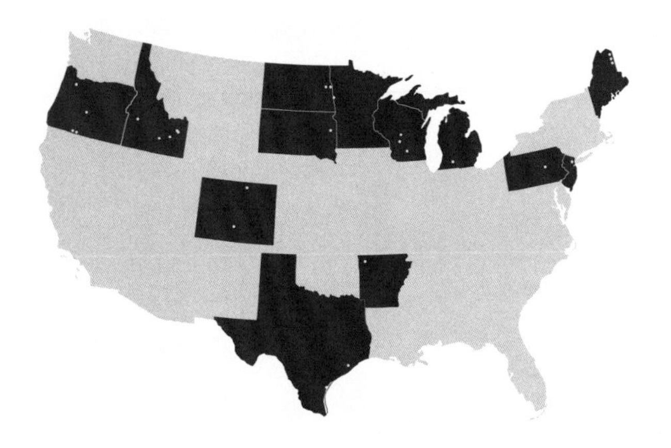

MAJOR WHITE POTATO-PRODUCING STATES (2016 CROP VALUE)

IDAHO	$968,274,000
WASHINGTON	$813,313,000
WISCONSIN	$322,944,000
CALIFORNIA	$265,305,000
NORTH DAKOTA	$222,480,000
COLORADO	$213,466,000
OREGON	$181,313,000
MAINE	$173,800,000
MICHIGAN	$173,604,000
MINNESOTA	$152,040,000

Source: USDA Potatoes 2016 Summary

Because of how widespread the potato industry is, twenty senators and dozens of Congressional representatives speak for its interests, pushing for policies like allowing schools to serve french fries as "vegetables" every day of the week. So who speaks for children's health? We have to. And we should eat more sweet potatoes instead; they're delicious and have more fiber and vitamins than white potatoes.

WHOLE ROASTED SWEET POTATOES

Yes, I really am going to give you a recipe for cooking plain old sweet potatoes, even though the basic instructions could easily fit in a tweet. But the recipe deserves a place here—after all, what other vegetable tastes this good when you've done so little to it? So yes, follow this no-chop, no-peel method to make my in-skin mash-ups (page 122–123) or whipped sweet potatoes (page 119–121). Or just bask in the glory of the sweet, creamy flesh with a little salt and butter—my favorite way to eat them.

SERVES 4
Active time: 10 MINUTES
Start to finish: 1¼ HOURS

4 to 6 medium sweet potatoes, scrubbed well and poked all over with a fork

1. Preheat the oven to 425°F. Line a baking sheet with parchment paper.

2. Put the sweet potatoes on the baking sheet with a little space between each one. Roast, without doing a thing to them, until the taut skin collapses slightly and you can slide a butter knife through the thickest part of the flesh with no resistance, 45 minutes to 1¼ hours, depending on their size.

WHIPPED SWEET POTATOES, THREE WAYS

Whipping roasted sweet potato flesh in the food processor transforms it from rustic to elegant, incorporating a little air to lighten the texture while playing up its creamy texture. The three ideas you'll see here have one thing in common: They include something tangy to balance the sweetness. Take the idea in whatever flavor directions you like, using whatever acidic component you have on hand—buttermilk, sour cream, orange or lemon juice, or mild vinegars are all great. From there, you can up the ante with something fresh, spicy, salty, or a combination. I like to pick elements that match the tart ingredient. If you're using lime juice, for instance, think cilantro and maybe chopped canned chipotles in adobo. If sour cream is providing the tang, think chives and bacon.

WHIPPED CRÈME FRAÎCHE-HERB

SWEET POTATO PUREE

You can't go wrong melting butter into steamy sweet potatoes, but if you can get your hands on crème fraîche, get ready to taste something even better. The French cultured cream tastes like a hybrid of butter and tangy sour cream. Lemon zest perks things up, and herbs keep things interesting—woodsy sage if you're in a cold-weather mood, or dill, which adds a grassy flavor that reminds me of springtime in Vienna. If you can't get crème fraîche, you can use sour cream instead. It won't be quite as rich, but it's still plenty delicious.

SERVES 4 TO 6
Active time: 15 MINUTES
Start to finish: 15 MINUTES

2½ pounds sweet potatoes (3 or 4 medium), roasted (opposite) and cooled

¾ cup crème fraîche

A few big pinches of thinly sliced fresh sage leaves or small handful of roughly chopped fresh dill

2 teaspoons grated lemon zest

Kosher salt

Peel the sweet potatoes and transfer the flesh to a food processor or a large bowl. Add the crème fraîche, half of the sage or dill, lemon zest, and ½ to 1 teaspoon salt. Process or whip with a sturdy whisk until smooth and slightly fluffy. Season with salt to taste. Top with the remaining sage or dill.

MAPLE-CIDER VINEGAR

SWEET POTATO PUREE

Just a little maple syrup plays up the the potato's complex-tasting sugars, and vinegar and pepper flakes prevent sweetness fatigue.

SERVES 4
Active time: 15 MINUTES
Start to finish: 15 MINUTES

2½ pounds sweet potatoes (3 or 4 medium), roasted (page 118) and cooled slightly

¼ cup maple syrup

¼ cup apple cider vinegar

1 teaspoon dried red pepper flakes

Kosher salt

Peel the sweet potatoes and transfer the flesh to a food processor or a large bowl. In a bowl, combine the maple syrup, vinegar, pepper flakes, and ½ to 1 teaspoon salt. Process or whip the potato with a sturdy whisk until smooth and slightly fluffy, adding half the maple-vinegar mixture. Season with more salt or maple vinegar to taste.

GOAT CHEESE-HERB

SWEET POTATO PUREE

When sweet potatoes and tangy goat cheese join forces, the result is so good you can pretty much stop there. But I like to add lemon zest—which adds the flavor of the fruit but not its tartness—and a handful of whatever fresh herbs I've got on hand.

SERVES 4
Active time: 15 MINUTES
Start to finish: 15 MINUTES

2½ pounds sweet potatoes (3 or 4 medium), roasted (page 118) and cooled slightly

½ cup soft goat cheese

Handful of coarsely chopped mixed fresh herbs, such as parsley, cilantro, tarragon, and marjoram

1 teaspoon grated lemon zest

Kosher salt

Peel the sweet potatoes and transfer the flesh to a food processor or a large bowl. Add the goat cheese, herbs, lemon zest, and ½ to ¾ teaspoon salt. Process or whip with a sturdy whisk until smooth and slightly fluffy. Season with salt to taste.

IN-SKIN MASH-UPS

This is a staple at my table: roasted sweet potatoes, slit on top to reveal their striking orange flesh, which I mash and fluff with a fork. To this foundation, I introduce a rotating cast of toppings, including these three winners. Take a look and you'll notice a pattern—there's always plenty of salt, something rich, and something acidic to keep all that natural sweetness in check. If you want to invent your own combination of toppings, use these three elements as a guideline and you'll do great.

BROWN BUTTER-ORANGE JUICE

SWEET POTATO MASH-UP

Some tricks from the pros don't translate easily to the home kitchen. (Leave the deep-frying and flambéeing to the people with fire suppression systems.) Brown butter, though, should be in every cook's arsenal. In my time at restaurants, I've melted virtual bathtubs of butter, patiently watching as it bubbled, frothed, and took on a golden-brown color and bolder, richer flavor as its nutty aroma filled the room. At home, it's a great way to make a little butter go a long way. Spike it with orange juice and you've got next-level stuff to drizzle on sweet potatoes that tames their sweetness with fat and acid.

SERVES 4 TO 6
Active time: 5 MINUTES
Start to finish: 1¼ HOURS

4 to 6 Whole Roasted Sweet Potatoes (page 118)

6 tablespoons (¾ stick) unsalted butter, cut into chunks

⅓ cup fresh orange juice

Kosher salt

1. While the sweet potatoes are roasting, put the butter in a light-colored heavy skillet. (The light color helps you keep track of the butter's color as it cooks.) Set it over medium heat and let the butter melt and bubble, stirring occasionally. Once it starts getting foamy, pay especially close attention to the color, pushing the foam aside frequently so you can spot when it turns golden brown, about 10 minutes from the time you turned on the stove.

2. Immediately pour the butter into a medium heatproof bowl, then stir in the orange juice and ¼ to ½ teaspoon salt.

3. Make a lengthwise slit in the top of each potato and mash a generous pinch of salt into the flesh with a fork. Spoon on the dressing.

BACON VINAIGRETTE

SWEET POTATO MASH-UP

You'll probably start drizzling this insanely easy bacon dressing on *everything*, but let's start with this sweet potato. The starchy flesh soaks up the vinaigrette and delivers smoky, porky flavor with each bite.

SERVES 4 TO 6
Active time: 5 MINUTES
Start to finish: 1¼ HOURS

4 to 6 Whole Roasted Sweet Potatoes (page 118)

6 ounces bacon slices

3 tablespoons sherry or apple cider vinegar

Kosher salt

1. While the sweet potatoes are roasting, cut the bacon into about ½-inch pieces and put it in a medium skillet. Cook over medium heat, stirring occasionally, until it releases its fat and turns brown and crisp, 8 to 10 minutes. Remove the skillet from the heat, then stir or whisk in the vinegar and ¼ to ½ teaspoon salt.

2. Make a lengthwise slit in the top of each potato and mash a generous pinch of salt into the flesh with a fork. Spoon on the dressing.

HERBED SOUR CREAM

SWEET POTATO MASH-UP

The combo of sour cream, chives, and potatoes is classic. But at home, I'd rather have my potatoes baked than fried, and I'll take a sweet potato over a Russet any day. Lively lemon and extra herbs make a near-perfect pairing even better.

SERVES 4 TO 6
Active time: 5 MINUTES
Start to finish: 1¼ HOURS

4 to 6 Whole Roasted Sweet Potatoes (page 118)

¾ cup sour cream

2 tablespoons thinly sliced fresh chives

1 tablespoon chopped fresh tarragon or thyme leaves

1 tablespoon fresh lemon juice

Kosher salt

1. While the sweet potatoes are roasting, combine the sour cream, chives, tarragon, lemon juice, and ¼ to ½ teaspoon salt in a small bowl and stir well.

2. Make a lengthwise slit in the top of each potato and mash a generous pinch of salt into the flesh with a fork. Spoon on the sour cream.

BACON VINAIGRETTE

BROWN BUTTER–ORANGE JUICE DRESSING

HERBED SOUR CREAM

SWEET POTATOES IN A HURRY

Roasted sweet potatoes often graced the First Family's dinner table. Yet even though roasting takes almost zero effort, it does take time. So when my day job as a policy advisor left me behind on dinner prep, I resorted to a highly sophisticated culinary technique for getting sweet potatoes ready fast: Cut them into small pieces and cook them in a pan. A few minutes of prep saves you almost an hour of cooking time. I use some of that stolen time to take the golden-brown cubes in three awesome directions. The same sweet potato–cooking principles apply: Make sure to balance their sugary quality with salt, acid, or even something pleasantly bitter, like wilted greens.

SPINACH, CURRANTS, PINE NUTS, AND BALSAMIC

SAUTÉED SWEET POTATOES

Spinach wilts in no time, adding color and flavor to the sweet, starchy cubes. An Italian-inspired trio of deliciousness does the rest—dried currants or golden raisins punctuate the potatoes' natural sweetness, toasted pine nuts add richness and crunch, and balsamic vinegar provides the acid that balances it all.

SERVES 4 TO 6
Active time: 20 MINUTES
Start to finish: 20 MINUTES

3 tablespoons extra-virgin olive oil

2½ pounds sweet potatoes (4 medium), peeled and cut into ½-inch cubes

Kosher salt

6 ounces baby spinach

½ cup dried currants or golden raisins

¼ cup pine nuts, toasted

2 tablespoons balsamic vinegar

1. Heat the oil in a large heavy skillet with a lid over medium-high heat until it shimmers, then stir in the sweet potatoes and ½ to ¾ teaspoon of salt. Cover and cook, stirring occasionally and lowering the heat if the potatoes take on color too quickly. If the potatoes are browned but not yet soft, add ¼ cup water to the pan and cook until evaporated. Repeat as needed until the potatoes are tender, 12 to 15 minutes total.

2. Add the spinach, gently tossing until wilted, 2 to 3 minutes. Stir in the currants, pine nuts, and balsamic and season with salt to taste.

APPLE AND LEEK
SAUTÉED SWEET POTATOES

To give this dish a touch of French flavor without the fuss, I look to leeks, which deserve way more attention that they get. Cooked in just enough butter, they take on a silky texture and subtle sweetness that's onion-like but more delicate. Apple brings a little tartness and crunch to contrast the chunks of sweet potato.

SERVES 4 TO 6
Active time: 25 MINUTES
Start to finish: 25 MINUTES

2 large leeks, white and pale green parts only, thinly sliced crosswise

3 tablespoons unsalted butter

Kosher salt

2½ pounds sweet potatoes (4 medium), peeled and cut into ½-inch cubes

1 tablespoon extra-virgin olive oil

1 large tart apple, such as Granny Smith

1 teaspoon chopped fresh thyme leaves

1. Toss the leeks gently in a bowl of cold water, letting any sand and grit fall to the bottom of the bowl. Use your hands to scoop the leeks into a kitchen towel–lined bowl to drain.

2. Heat 2 tablespoons butter in a large heavy skillet with a lid over medium heat until hot. Stir in the leeks and sprinkle on ½ to ¾ teaspoon of salt. Cover and cook, stirring occasionally, until the leeks are wilted, about 3 minutes. Stir in the sweet potatoes and the oil, cover again, and cook, stirring occasionally and lowering the heat if they take on color too quickly, until the potatoes are golden brown and tender, 10 to 12 minutes.

3. Peel and core the apple and cut it into ¼-inch cubes. Stir it into the skillet along with the remaining butter and thyme. Cook, stirring, until the apple is tender but still a little crunchy, 3 to 4 minutes. Season with salt to taste.

GINGER AND SCALLION

SAUTÉED SWEET POTATOES

Scallions, ginger, and garlic are the holy trinity of aromatics in Cantonese cooking. They transform whatever they touch into something tasty—even when it's something they don't traditionally end up with, like the humble sweet potato. If you like heat, red pepper flakes are great here.

SERVES 4 TO 6
Active time: 25 MINUTES
Start to finish: 25 MINUTES

3 tablespoons vegetable oil

2½ pounds sweet potatoes (4 medium), peeled and cut into ½-inch cubes

Kosher salt

1 bunch of scallions, roots trimmed, thinly sliced

2 tablespoons peeled and finely chopped fresh ginger

2 garlic cloves, finely chopped

Toasted sesame oil to taste

1 lime, halved

1. Heat the vegetable oil in a large heavy skillet with a lid over medium-high heat until it shimmers, then stir in the sweet potatoes and sprinkle on ½ to ¾ teaspoon of salt. Cover and cook, stirring occasionally and lowering the heat if the potatoes take on color too quickly, until golden brown and tender, 10 to 12 minutes.

2. Stir in the scallions, ginger, and garlic and cook, stirring frequently, until the garlic and ginger are golden, 3 to 5 minutes. Remove it from the heat and stir in up to 1 tablespoon of sesame oil. Season with lime and more salt to taste.

BE A BETTER MEAT EATER

Just about every summer Friday at the White House, around 5 p.m., I'd set up a beat-up old grill near the North Portico. I'd light wood charcoal, let the grates get screaming hot, and lay on a few steaks. As the meat sizzled, reporters would invariably file out of the press briefing room, smiling as they located the source of the unmistakable fragrance of caramelizing beef. Without fail, someone would crack, "Hey, Sam, what time's dinner?" They'd just finished grilling the president (by way of his press secretary, at least) and now they wanted some of what I was grilling. So I'd holler back with a smile: "Whenever the president told you to come by."

Sometimes I'd cook hanger or strip steak. Yet like most wise people, President Obama is a rib eye fan. So most Fridays I'd grab a few thick-cut slabs flecked with white fat, dust them with nothing more than salt and pepper, hit them with a little oil, and char them until a deep-brown crust encased a perfect pink. As the rib eyes rested, I'd finish cooking whatever vegetables we'd harvested from the garden that day; then I'd cut the steaks against the grain into thick slices. There's nothing better.

A love letter to steak might not be what you'd expect at the beginning of a chapter encouraging you to be a better meat eater by, in part, eating less beef. But I don't come to this issue as someone blind to the pleasures of a good burger or pot of braised short ribs or, well, a steak. I'm not going to give up meat. I don't think we have to. But we do have to make some changes.

There's no denying that raising livestock—chickens, pigs, cows, and the rest—is a much less efficient way of feeding the world than growing fruits, vegetables, and grains. Every pound of meat produced requires large amounts of grain—and all the fossil fuels, fertilizers, and water it takes to produce that feed. This wouldn't be as big a problem if we didn't produce meat on the scale we do. Animals raised for food outnumber the world's population several times over. They require 30 percent of the earth's surface, 10 percent of its water, and produce about

15 percent of greenhouse gas emissions, including methane gas, which traps twenty-five times more heat than carbon dioxide.

So if the meat industry is a problem, the beef industry is the main culprit. Beef is dramatically more inefficient to produce than pork or chicken, and cows are by far the biggest contributors to those alarming stats. And while beef isn't poison—as some make it out to be—we're eating more of it than is good for our health.

When President Obama told me he wanted to institute Steak Fridays, he wasn't trying to make a statement about climate change. He just wanted to eat less red meat, to do a little better. But as someone who loves to eat and in particular loves to take down a good steak, he faced the same dilemma that so many of us do: How do you make meaningful change without changing everything? In other words, how do you do better?

The key is to figure out what realistic progress looks like for you. That's what we did for the president. Like a lot of guys of his generation, he was used to eating beef several times a week, so we decided to make beef an occasional food, and that would mean Friday was steak night. (Everyone deserves a reward for getting through the work week, but especially the leader of the free world.) Designating one night a week for this treat meant that for the other six, we weren't eating beef. For some people, this might not seem like a big sacrifice, and for others, it might seem almost unbearably strict. But again, the point is to make *progress* relative to what you do now. Following this rule (even with an occasional exception), the president cut his beef consumption dramatically. And if everyone did a little of this, we'd be making real progress. In 2015, Americans ate about 25 billion pounds of beef. That's seventy-seven pounds of beef per person per year—and realistically, that number is even greater when you consider that infants and children probably aren't wolfing down the average pound and a half of beef per week.

For the rest of his meals, I made the president fish, chicken, and pork to go with lots of vegetables and grains—all of which are decidedly better, all things considered, than beef. The key was making that food taste really good, so good he didn't even notice he was eating less beef. It's the same advice I try to follow myself and the same advice I have for you.

To help get you there, I share recipes for dishes that will make it easier to stick to your guns.

To go a little further, I provide tips, techniques, and other tools that aim to make you a flexible, more confident cook. You'll find not just recipes for my favorite sustainable seafood, but a walk-through of how to cook perfect fish fillets and easy ways to sauce them. I give you both my go-to roasted chicken and slow-roasted pork shoulder recipes and also tasty ideas for what to do with the leftovers, so one night of cooking keeps you fed for days. Finally, I give one awesome, foolproof recipe for rib eye steak, my choice for when the time for indulgence arrives, plus four sauces that make a good thing even better.

EAT
MORE
FISH

IF I TOLD YOU there was a place where an incredibly sophisticated operation had developed a way to deliver a never-ending supply of good food without machines, fertilizers, or even seeds, you might think I was fantasizing . . . or pitching a new start-up.

But this is not a vision of the future. This is what we have right now—millions upon millions of miles of oceans, seas, and rivers that foster constantly regenerating populations of beautiful, delicious fish, an entirely sustainable food source full of lean protein and healthy fats. If we start making a few better decisions, we can keep it this way. If not, this miracle will become a thing of the past.

The solution, oddly enough, is to eat more fish. If we replace even some of the meat we eat with fish, we will go a long way toward reducing the enormous impact meat production has on climate change. (The supply chain of seafood has almost no effect on climate change in comparison to meat, though some meats are better than others, as we'll discuss later.)

At the same time, we need to eat more of the *better kinds* of fish. And admittedly, the choices to be made aren't exactly as simple as choosing wild over farmed. Some species are overfished and nearing collapse or extinction, which could send the whole ecosystem out of whack. (Bad things happen when the natural balance of predators and prey gets thrown off because we've eaten a whole link of the food chain out of existence.) And unlike the chicken and pig, of course, seafood isn't one animal. It's a category of creature—hundreds of species that live in waters around the world. The practices that make all the difference vary by fishery and farm and aren't always reflected on signs and labels at the average market. Keeping track of all that would take a ton of work. Here's the good news: Someone has already done that work for you.

No, not me. The Monterey Bay Aquarium, whose Seafood Watch research project is your best guide to shopping for seafood. They even have an app for your phone. To follow their guidance, you'll need a little more info than a restaurant menu or fish market provides. You may have to ask a few questions—where the fish is from; which species is it (for example, is the tuna bluefin or albacore); and, if you can stomach sounding like *that* person, how was it caught? Seafood Watch rates different fish from different areas as "best choices," "good alternatives," or "avoid." When you can, choose sustainably or reasonably caught wild or farmed fish. When you can't, choose chicken.

When you can, choose sustainably or reasonably caught wild or farmed fish. When you can't, choose chicken.

Aside from their assistance, I've come up with some helpful, easy-to-remember strategies that can guide you in your quest to eat more of the good stuff. I also share some of my favorite ways to treat smart-choice seafood and tips to make you a more flexible cook, so you can go into a store confident that if they've got any fish that passes the test, you can cook it.

EAT MORE TYPES OF FISH

At first glance, the notion of buying thoughtfully probably sounds like a buzzkill: You shouldn't eat this! Don't buy that! But it can actually *expand* your options. Right now, more than half of the seafood we buy is tuna, salmon, and shrimp—this, when there are hundreds of varieties of seafood we can enjoy. Eating too much of too few fish creates an imbalance that threatens our fish supply. We're eating wild tuna at such a clip that species like bluefin are nearly extinct. While most of the salmon and shrimp we eat is farmed, their production relies heavily on wild fish like anchovies, herring, and sardines for feed. And even though both convert food to flesh at a more efficient rate than most meat, the sheer amount of salmon and shrimp we eat puts stress on the populations of those feeder fish, which throws ecosystems off balance. Shifting your focus from the Big Three will help restore equilibrium. It'll also introduce you to some seriously delicious fish.

GET LOW

In the absence of a good guide like Seafood Watch, there is a general rule that can help guide you toward sustainable seafood: Focus on those creatures that are low on the food chain. Small fish like anchovies, sardines, and mackerel are more plentiful than large fish and reproduce more quickly, so their populations are less likely to collapse. Bonus: Since they have shorter lifespans, these fish have less time to accumulate mercury and the other toxins that oblige FDA advisories. Double bonus: These fish taste *really* good and are packed with superhealthy fats.

BUY AMERICAN

No, not out of pure patriotic duty. No, not because wild shrimp netted in the Gulf of Mexico and salmon caught in Alaska taste amazing (though man, do they ever!). But because America has some of the best regulations on fishing and farming. And right now, more than 90 percent of the fish we eat come from elsewhere, primarily countries in Asia where the sorts of protocols that protect the local environment and wild populations are lax. American fisheries, of course, aren't exempt from poor practices. Still, buying fish raised or caught in waters around this country will generally guide you toward better choices.

EAT WILD *AND* FARMED

What fish to buy doesn't have an easy answer, but one thing's for sure: The question that has come to define the decision—wild or farmed?—turns out to be the wrong one, according to Paul Greenberg, author of *Four Fish: The Future of the Last Wild Food* and probably the most informed guy on the topic. Because, contrary to what you may have heard, there *are* good fish farms, and if we're going to increase our seafood consumption without wrecking our oceans, we're going to need to eat both responsibly-caught wild fish *and* well-raised farmed fish.

WILD Catching wild fish might sound romantic—a simple fisherman casting his line into the sea and pulling out dinner. But wild fish are caught today on a scale that's almost unimaginable. The technology has gotten to the point where it is possible to almost literally empty our oceans. And to stock our supermarkets with fillets and our freezers with fish sticks, many commercial operations fish indiscriminately. They pull tuna, cod, salmon, and many more from the water at a faster rate than they can reproduce, decimating their populations and snuffing the ability for their numbers to recover. They employ massive nets or lines that stretch for miles to catch a target fish, but end up ensnaring many other creatures, which are typically discarded. When caught responsibly, however, wild seafood truly is a renewable resource. And unlike farming vegetables or meat, catching wild fish requires no clearing of forests and has a carbon footprint of approximately zero. Seafood Watch can guide you toward creatures with healthy populations and speedy reproduction, those caught in waters where quotas are respected and enforced, and those caught through methods, like jigging and hook and line, that don't disturb underwater ecosystems.

FARMED Once upon a time, we hunted for our protein on land. As our population grew and animals became scarce, we turned to farming. Now the same thing is happening with the creatures of the sea. If we want to eat more seafood without destroying wild populations, farming is the key.

It's true that the methods used by many fish farms have proved problematic. For one, two of the main fish we raise through aquaculture—salmon and shrimp—happen to require huge amounts of small wild fish for food. In other words, to prop up two sea creatures we love to eat, we decimate many others, undermining ocean ecosystems in the process. Some operations rely instead on feed made from corn and soy, which produces nutrient-deficient seafood and supports the same agricultural products that feed our system's reliance on synthetic fertilizers. To maximize their yields, some farms cram fish in pens, pools, and tanks, employing antibiotics, disinfectants, and other chemicals to prevent the spread of disease aggravated by overcrowding. Runoff from these operations—antibiotics, escaped fish, stray feed, and waste to name a few—disturbs the ocean environment nearby.

But there is some good news. Sustainable aquaculture operations are growing in numbers. They might employ tanks separated from surrounding waters so the fish and waste won't affect nearby ecosystems. They might focus on omnivores that can go vegetarian, like catfish, and perhaps best of all, bivalves like clams, oysters, and mussels, some of the most sustainable seafood you can eat. They require no feed at all since they eat microscopic marine plants that they filter from water. The more we buy responsibly farmed fish, the more we support the operations that will allow us to continue enjoying the fruits of the sea.

THE TROUBLE WITH COOKING FISH AT THE WHITE HOUSE

It was 6:22 p.m., and I was in the White House Residence kitchen, waiting for the call. My buddies Carter and Vaughn, longtime butlers and two of the funniest guys I know, unleashed a steady stream of banter, cracking me up as usual—part of the daily dinner ritual. A skillet was on the stove. I'd seasoned sea bass fillets and they were ready to go. When the phone finally rang, I got my ten-minute warning from the guys in the West Wing with eyes on the boss: "Poppa's on his way." It was time for the high-wire act of cooking fish for the president of the United States.

Most days, I didn't need advance notice. Somehow, the president managed to get to the table on time at 6:30. And even when he was a little late, dinner didn't suffer. I'd have everything ready, keeping chicken or pork chops warm and readying vegetables or grain for a final toss in a pan. But the nights the president was having fish, a heads-up was essential.

Fish cooks quickly, so you can get it on the table even on those days when time is short. The problem is, fish tastes best just after it leaves the pan, not the warmer drawer. It's the kind of food you want to finish cooking once everyone's seated at the table and ready to dig in. Hence the ten-minute warning. That way, I could avoid both keeping the president waiting for the fish and, nearly as bad, keeping the fish waiting for the president.

As soon as I got word, I cranked up the stove, got the skillet and some oil good and hot, and added the fillet. A few minutes later, the phone rang again: The guys had guessed wrong—the boss was actually on his way to the South Lawn to walk the loop with his chief of staff, as he sometimes did when he had an important decision to make. So I rushed over to the stove to rescue the fish. Minutes later, another call. The president was approaching the elevator that took him to the Residence. Phew, I thought, as I put the fillet back into the oil. Then, yeah, you guessed it. *Ring ring*—sorry, he got called into the Oval Office. That poor fillet. By the time he had arrived, I'd finished cooking the fish (not my best work), ate it myself, and chased down another fillet. It didn't hit the pan until I saw the boss's face.

THE BLUEPRINT

SEARING FISH

Fish comes in many varieties, all with different flavors and textures. It's just one reason I love eating fish, but it also explains why many people are reluctant to cook fish at home. Someone might be confident baking salmon, but baffled by barramundi. When faced with fillets of rockfish at the market, most might wonder if it's best to roast, sear, steam, broil, or fry it before giving up and buying the salmon. The thing is, eating more kinds of fish, not just the few we're used to, is an important part of eating sustainably.

Now, it's true that fish lend themselves to many different cooking methods. But in the interest of keeping things simple and giving you the confidence to cook whatever comes your way, I want to share with you my method for preparing virtually any fish fillet—a good, hard sear on one side.

WHAT YOU'LL NEED

Fish fillets and flour

A heavy pan wide enough to hold the fillets without crowding

Kosher salt

Canola or grapeseed oil

A thin spatula, or even better, a proper fish spatula (for easy flipping)

1. Get whatever you're serving with the fish—the rice, the salad—ready to go.

2. Grab a heavy pan and set it over medium-high heat. If your piece of fish is an inch or more thick, preheat the oven to 375°F, too. Give the pan a couple minutes to get good and hot—this helps keep it from sticking.

3. Pat the fillets dry with paper towels and season both sides with salt. If the fish has skin, lay it skin-side down on a plate of flour to coat it in an even, thin layer.

4. Pour a healthy slick of neutral oil, like canola or grapeseed (extra-virgin olive oil will smoke like crazy) into the pan and swirl it to coat.

5. Add the fillets (skin-side down, if applicable) and cook, without touching them (seriously, don't do it!), until you see a golden-brown border around the fillets. One exception: If the fish curls, use a spatula to gently but firmly press it down so the fillets lie flat. Do this a couple of times and the fish should stay flat without further pressing.

6. Carefully flip the fish (it'll release easily now that it's brown and enough moisture has evaporated) and cook briefly just until it's fully cooked (see opposite). If it's thick, transfer the pan to the oven to finish cooking for a few minutes. Eat right away.

IS IT DONE?

Chefs can tell when fish is done with the prod of a finger or even a glance at the flesh. But for many home cooks, knowing when fish is ready presents a challenge that can keep them from even trying. So here's my first tip: Check the fish frequently. As soon as a thin sharp knife or skewer inserted into the thickest part of the fillet encounters no resistance, the fish is definitely done. Err on the side of underdone—you can always keep cooking, but you can't uncook. In fact, I prefer most fish a little underdone, and if my skewer finds a touch of resistance, it's usually perfect for me.

If you're unsure, there's no shame in using a knife to slice open and peek inside the thickest part, even if that means sacrificing picture-perfect presentation. If the flesh is opaque or just barely translucent in the very center, you're good. Keep in mind it'll continue cooking once it leaves the hot pan or oven. There are a few exceptions. Salmon and arctic char, for example, are best medium rare, when the center still has an orange hue rather than the pale pink color of fully cooked flesh. Tuna is best rare, when the center is warm but still raw, to medium rare.

FISH, SAUCED

Nice fish needs little more than a sprinkle of salt, a trip in a hot pan, and a squeeze of lemon. But whipping up a simple sauce can liven things up and take any basic fish recipe in different directions. Here are a few sauce and condiment ideas that take mere minutes to make.

* Mix about ½ cup plain **yogurt** with a squeeze of **lemon,** a big pinch of salt, and as much coarsely chopped fresh **tarragon, cilantro,** and/or **parsley** as you want.

* Mix about ¼ cup **soy sauce** with a big squeeze of **lemon,** a pinch of **sugar,** a healthy amount of grated fresh **ginger,** and a little **sesame oil.**

* Mix a handful of pretty finely chopped **fresh herbs** (anything except sage) with a generous pinch of salt, a squeeze of **lemon,** and just enough **oil** to moisten the herbs.

* Mix a medium bowl's worth of fairly finely chopped **tomatoes, cucumbers, radishes,** and **white onions** with a drizzle of **olive oil** and a small handful of chopped fresh **cilantro** or **parsley.** Season aggressively with salt and **lime juice.**

* Mix the juice of a couple **limes** with an equal amount of **fish sauce,** a pinch of **sugar,** and a small handful of chopped fresh **cilantro.** Stir in finely chopped **jalapeño, serrano,** or **Thai chiles** to taste.

* Melt a good pat of **butter** in a small skillet over medium heat. Add an equal amount of **olive oil** and 2 or 3 thinly sliced **garlic** cloves. Cook until the garlic is golden brown, add a tablespoon or two of **capers** or **chopped olives,** and cook for a minute. Remove it from heat and squeeze in plenty of **lemon** juice.

* Drizzle on **spicy aïoli** (page 61).

SHALLOW-FRIED CATFISH

WITH COLLARDS, POBLANO SALSA, AND RED BEANS AND RICE

While her husband maintained a punishing campaign schedule, Michelle Obama was juggling a job, showing up at occasional campaign events, and caring for her daughters. So she was pumped to have me around to make dinner a few nights a week. Barack didn't quite share her enthusiasm. He was always friendly and gracious, but clearly not 100 percent on board—he never saw himself as a guy who would have a private chef.

So when I got word one day that Barack had the night off to eat at home, I knew I had to make him a meal that would win a skeptic over. I decided to use wholesome ingredients—brown rice, beans, collard greens, and fish—and focus on making them taste great. Because the stakes felt high, I pulled out the stops: Bacon found its way into the vegetables and grains. I breaded and shallow-fried the fish to a golden crisp. These might seem like hallmarks of unhealthy food, but bacon and fried foods aren't evil. It's just that we eat them too much. An important dinner like this one was a great time for a little indulgence.

Barack got home late, and it was just him and his plate of food in the kitchen. "Solid!" he said after his first bite. "Man, this is some tasty stuff." I would come to learn that "solid" is exactly what you wanted to hear from the man. It was a sign he was truly satisfied. As he ate, we had the first of countless conversations about politics—one that, after all that's happened since, I'm pretty sure he doesn't remember. But for me, it was a moment I'll never forget.

The salsa and the greens can all be made a day in advance.

SERVES 4
Active time: **1 HOUR**
Start to finish: **1¾ HOURS**

FOR THE POBLANO SALSA

3 medium poblano peppers

½ cup finely chopped red onion

1 cup very coarsely chopped fresh cilantro

Finely grated zest from 2 limes

1 tablespoon fresh lime juice

Kosher salt

3 tablespoons vegetable oil

1. MAKE THE POBLANO SALSA: Turn two gas stove burners to medium high. (If your stove is electric, you can approximate this by using a baking sheet under the broiler.) Set the poblano peppers on the burner grates over the flames and cook, flipping occasionally, until the skin is completely black and blistered, 8 to 10 minutes. Transfer them to a bowl and cover it with a plate. Let the peppers chill out until cool enough to handle, about 15 minutes. Use your fingers or the back of a knife to rub off the skins. Cut out the stems, then slit the peppers open and scrape out the seeds. Coarsely chop the flesh and put it in a blender along with the onion, cilantro, lime zest and juice, and ½ to ¾ teaspoon of salt. Blend to a coarse puree; then, with the motor running, pour in the oil and continue to blend until well combined. Season with salt to taste. Transfer to a serving bowl and set aside.

recipe continues

FOR THE COLLARDS

¼ pound bacon slices, cut into about 1-inch pieces, or 2 tablespoons olive oil

2 garlic cloves, thinly sliced

1 large bunch collard greens, bottom 1 inch of stems trimmed

2½ cups low-sodium chicken stock

¼ cup red wine vinegar, plus more to taste

Kosher salt

2. MAKE THE COLLARD GREENS: Put the bacon (or olive oil if you're using it), and garlic in a large heavy pot over medium heat and cook, stirring occasionally, until the garlic turns light golden, 2 to 8 minutes. Cut the collard leaves crosswise into strips an inch or so wide. Add the collards, stock, vinegar, and ½ teaspoon of salt and bring to a simmer over medium-high heat. Simmer until the collards are tender, 25 to 45 minutes, depending on your preference (I like collards with a little chew) and how tough they are to begin with. Season with more salt and vinegar to taste. Keep the collards warm.

FOR THE CATFISH

½ cup all-purpose flour

2 teaspoons smoked paprika

Kosher salt

2 large eggs, lightly beaten

¾ cup unseasoned dried bread crumbs

4 catfish fillets (½ pound each), patted dry

About 1 cup vegetable oil, for shallow-frying

Red Beans and Rice (page 268), for serving

3. FOR THE CATFISH: Preheat the oven to the lowest possible temperature. Stir the flour, paprika, and 1 teaspoon of salt together on a large plate. Whisk the eggs in a large shallow bowl. Put the bread crumbs on another large plate.

4. Season the fish all over with 1 teaspoon salt. Working with one fillet at a time, put the fish in the seasoned flour and turn to coat in a thin layer, shaking off any excess. Put each fillet in the egg mixture and turn to coat it well. Let any excess egg drip off, then put each fillet in the bread crumbs, turn to coat well, and remove it to a plate.

5. Pour the oil into a large heavy skillet to a depth of about ¼ inch. Heat over medium heat until shimmering hot. Carefully set 2 fillets in the oil and fry, flipping once, until golden brown all over and cooked through, 10 to 12 minutes total. Transfer the catfish to a paper towel–lined plate to drain, season to taste with salt, and keep warm in the oven while you cook the remaining fillets.

6. Make plates of the collards, red beans and rice, and catfish. Serve the poblano salsa in a bowl alongside.

PAN-SEARED WHOLE SARDINES

WITH ESCAROLE, GRAPEFRUIT, AND GREEN OLIVES

Sardines don't only come in cans (though I love the ones that do!). These silver-skinned beauties are cheap, super flavorful, and sustainable (see page 137). That they hold their own in the company of assertive ingredients like briny olives, sweet-tart grapefruit, and awesomely bitter escarole is yet another plus. A good fishmonger will do the cleaning for you. Just give the sardines a last-minute rinse, running your fingers alongside the skin to loosen any lingering scales.

SERVES 4 TO 6
Active time: 30 MINUTES
Start to finish: 30 MINUTES

2 grapefruit
Extra-virgin olive oil, as needed
White wine vinegar, to taste
Kosher salt
1 small head of escarole, torn into bite-sized pieces
12 whole fresh sardines (about 3 pounds total), scaled and gutted
½ cup all-purpose flour
1 cup pitted green olives, coarsely chopped

1. Trim the tops and bottoms of the grapefruit with a sharp knife. Working from top to bottom and following the curve of the fruit, carve off the peel and pith to expose the flesh. Working over a big bowl, cut each grapefruit segment from the membrane and add it to the bowl. When you're done, squeeze the juice from the membranes into the bowl, then discard the membranes. Stir in 2 to 3 tablespoons of olive oil, the vinegar, and salt to taste.

2. Scatter the escarole over a serving platter.

3. Season the sardines all over with salt. Spread the flour on a plate. One by one, set the sardines skin-side down in the flour to coat lightly on one side.

4. Heat 2 tablespoons of the oil in a large heavy skillet over medium-high heat until it shimmers. Cook the sardines in batches to avoid crowding the skillet, adding more oil as necessary. If you've butterflied the sardines (see opposite), cook them skin-side down until golden, about 3 minutes, then flip them to cook through, about 30 seconds. If the sardines are whole, cook them until golden on one side, about 3 minutes, then flip and cook about 3 minutes more.

5. Transfer the hot sardines to the platter with the escarole. Scatter the olives and grapefruit segments over the fish. Drizzle on the grapefruit juice remaining in the bowl and season with salt.

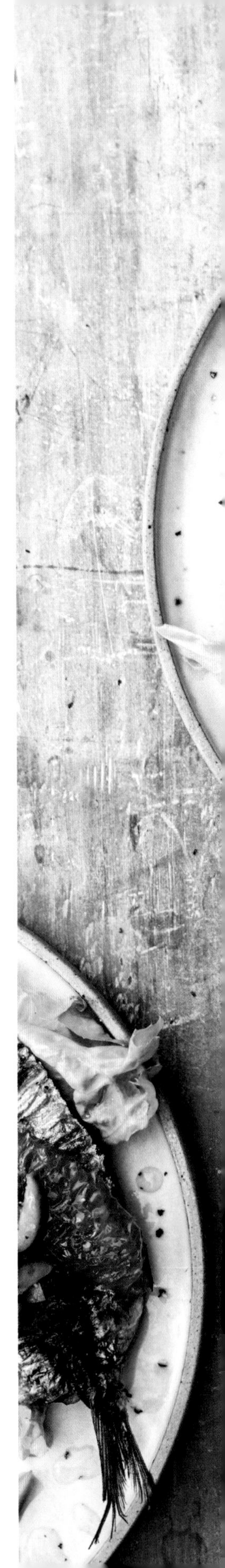

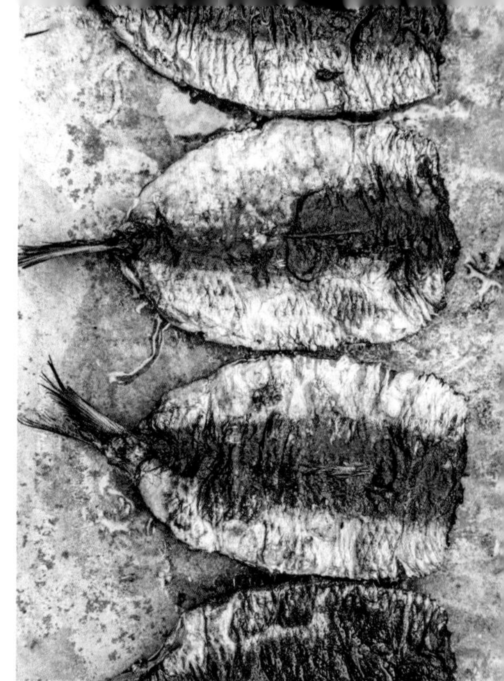

BUTTERFLYING SARDINES: For an extra-cool presentation (and a boneless eating experience), consider butterflying the sardines. Here's how: For each sardine, cut just behind the gills to remove the head. Set the sardine with the slit belly against the cutting board and the backbone facing up. Firmly press down against the backbone, starting at the front and working your way toward the tail, until the sardine lies flat. Flip it flesh-side up, grab the tip of the backbone, and firmly but carefully pull it away from the flesh, using your free hand to steady the fish against the cutting board so the backbone brings as little flesh with it as possible. Finally, run a finger along the flesh and use your fingers or tweezers to remove any stray bones.

SARDINE SMASH TOASTS

Now this is my kind of fast food. You're home and you're hungry, so you rub a cut clove of garlic on warm crusty bread, pop open a can of sardines, grab a couple of simple additions for acid and freshness, and you're set. It's good for you, it's good for the planet, and it's satisfying, too. Since sardines are naturally rich and usually come packed in oil, they don't require the gobs of mayo that canned tuna does.

SERVES 4
Active time: 10 MINUTES
Start to finish: 10 MINUTES

4 thick slices country-style bread

3 tablespoons extra-virgin olive oil, plus more as needed

1 garlic clove, cut in half

Two 3.75-ounce cans sardines in olive oil

½ cup diced cucumber

3 tablespoons fresh lemon juice

Small handful of coarsely chopped fresh parsley

Kosher salt

1. Drizzle the bread on both sides with the oil (about 1 teaspoon per side) and toast in a toaster oven or a 400°F oven, flipping once, until golden and crisp, 5 to 8 minutes. Let the toasts cool slightly, then rub the cut side of the garlic on the toasts. Cut the toasts in half.

2. Dump the sardines and their oil into a bowl. Add the the cucumber, lemon juice, and parsley. Add a little olive oil, if you like, mash it together lightly, then season with salt to taste. Scoop the mixture onto the toasts and serve.

STEAMED MUSSELS

WITH GARLIC, WHITE WINE, AND TOMATO

Mussels have so many things going for them: They cook quickly, they're relatively inexpensive, and they're as sustainable as can be. They're tasty, too—full of a clean, mild sea flavor that needs little more than a flavorful liquid, garlic, and a good sauce sopper like crusty bread or whole grains. The key is not overcooking them. Here's how: Instead of cooking them in the pot until all their shells have popped open, hang out at the stove with tongs ready, peeking often under the lid and plucking out mussels as soon as they open, so they stay plump and tender. Here's a classic preparation, and flip the page for some directions you can take them.

SERVES 2 TO 4
Active time: 30 MINUTES
Start to finish: 30 MINUTES

3 tablespoons extra-virgin olive oil

3 garlic cloves, thinly sliced

1 large shallot, thinly sliced

¼ to ½ teaspoon dried red pepper flakes, to taste

One 15-ounce can diced tomatoes, or 1 pound fresh tomatoes, cored and diced

½ cup dry white wine

4 dozen mussels, scrubbed well and stringy "beards" pulled off

Kosher salt

Big handful of coarsely chopped fresh parsley

1. Put a big bowl next to the stove. Heat the oil in a large pot or Dutch oven over medium heat until it shimmers. Add the garlic and shallots and cook, stirring frequently, until they're soft but not colored, about 2 minutes.

2. Stir in the pepper flakes and tomatoes, then add the white wine. Increase the heat to medium high, bring the wine to a boil, and cook for a minute or so. Add the mussels, cover the pot, and give it a good shake to distribute the mussels evenly. Grab tongs and get ready.

3. Cook, shaking the pot and peeking under the lid occasionally, until the first few mussels shells pop open. (Start checking after 3 minutes or so.) When they do, use the tongs to transfer them to the bowl. Keep cooking and plucking out mussels as they're done until they've all opened. (Any that don't open for a suspiciously long time after the rest are done are probably dead; throw them out.) Carefully taste the hot liquid left in the pot, add salt to taste, then add the mussels back to the pot to rewarm them for a few seconds. Turn off the heat, hit them with the parsley, and serve them right away in the pot.

MUSSEL (AND CLAM) VARIATIONS

Most of my favorite recipes for mussels follow the same formula and you can treat clams the same way. Once you know it, you can take them in any direction you want. Basically, you heat some fat (oil, butter, bacon), saute aromatic ingredients (garlic, scallions, ginger), and add some flavorful liquid (wine, stock, coconut milk). When it comes to a simmer, you add the shellfish, cover the pan, and cook them until the shells have popped open. Herbs are optional but encouraged. Here are a few combinations I love:

- Heat chopped bacon in a large pot until the fat renders and it begins to brown, saute leeks, and add white wine. Boil it for a minute, stir in a little Dijon mustard, and add the mussels.
- Heat olive oil in a large pot, saute a diced onion until soft, then saute a cup of two of corn kernels and a finely chopped serrano or jalapeño chile. Add fish stock and the juice of two or three lemons, then add the mussels. When they're done, top with lots of chopped basil.
- Heat chopped Spanish chorizo in a large pot until the fat renders and it begins to brown, saute a diced onion, and add beer. Boil it for a minute, add the mussels. When they're done, stir in a touch of sherry vinegar.

AN OPEN AND SHUT CASE

Mussels, clams, oysters, and other bivalves you buy in the shell aren't just sold fresh—they're sold alive. Occasionally, one or two kick the bucket on the way to the market. So check your stash for any whose shells are open. Squeeze them closed—if they stay closed, they're alive and good to cook. If they don't, toss them. Then, when you cook them, watch for any that don't open. You can give them a little more time on the heat (I like to remove the opened ones so they don't overcook), but if they stay stubbornly closed after a few more minutes, toss those, too.

GRILLED CLAMS

WITH SHISHITO PEPPERS AND LEMON

If you love the bold, briny sweetness of clams as much as I do, you'll be thrilled to know that they also happen to be close to perfect when it comes to sustainability. Farmed clams, which represent the vast majority on offer in markets, have approximately zero negative impact on the ocean ecosystem and, in fact, help to clean the water they're in.

While I'm all for cooking clams as I do mussels, in a covered pot on the stove, my favorite way is to grill them. I love watching as they steam themselves open, nabbing them with tongs the moment they do and carefully transporting them, precious juices and all, to a bowl. That way, no clams overcook and their juices pool, forming the sauce of a shellfish fan's dreams along with butter and lemon. You have a showstopper right there, but whenever I can find them, I char some shishito peppers—mild but flavor-packed green chiles that you eat whole—and toss them in the bowl, too.

SERVES 4 TO 6
Active time: 25 MINUTES
Start to finish: 25 MINUTES

3 tablespoons unsalted butter
2 garlic cloves, chopped (optional)
Dried red pepper flakes, to taste
3 dozen or so small, tender clams, such as littlenecks, soaked and scrubbed (see opposite)
1 pound shishito peppers, stems removed
1 lemon, halved
Kosher salt

1. Preheat a gas or charcoal grill to high heat. Put the butter in a heatproof bowl large enough to hold all the clams and peppers. (If using the garlic, heat it in a small saucepan with the butter over low heat until well softened, and pour it all into the bowl.) Add pepper flakes to taste.

2. Grill the clams and peppers in a single layer and have a pair of tongs ready. Cook the clams until they open wide, transferring them to the bowl as soon as they do, 10 to 15 minutes. Cook the shishito peppers, flipping them occasionally, until tender and charred, 8 to 10 minutes, transferring them to the bowl with the clams. Squeeze on enough lemon juice to brighten things up. Season with salt to taste—clams are often naturally salty, so you might not need much—and toss really well.

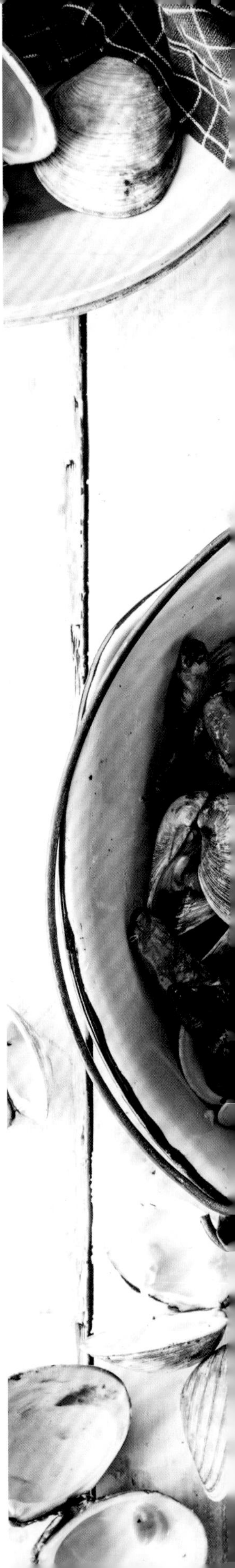

CLEANING CLAMS: Before you cook clams, submerge them in a bowl of cold water for an hour or so. The clams will release any grit into the water. Then give each one a quick scrub under running water and they're ready to go.

SHRIMP NOODLE BOWL

One typically hot, sticky day in Hanoi, the capital of Vietnam, I sat on a tiny red plastic stool on the sidewalk and hunched over a bowl of simple, steamy soup packed with noodles and shrimp. It was so good I gulped it down like ice water. I could never hope to replicate the splendor of that vendor's soup, which she'd probably made every day for decades, but when I got home, I couldn't help but try. While my version doesn't match hers, it's pretty damn good—especially if you use American Gulf shrimp, which are briny and sweet, like shrimp should be. They get bonus points for being better for you and the environment than the stuff shipped in from farming operations in Asia, which accounts for close to 90 percent of shrimp sold in the United States.

SERVES 4 TO 6
Active time: 20 MINUTES
Start to finish: 40 MINUTES

3 tablespoons vegetable oil

6 ounces shiitake mushrooms, stemmed and thinly sliced

1 pound baby bok choy, sliced

2 tablespoons peeled and finely chopped fresh ginger

2 garlic cloves, thinly sliced

1 quart low-sodium chicken stock

1 quart low-sodium fish stock (or more chicken stock)

4 ounces glass noodles (aka cellophane noodles or bean threads)

1¼ pounds large shrimp, peeled

Kosher salt

4 tablespoons fish sauce or soy sauce

Freshly ground black pepper

4 scallions, sliced

1 lime, cut into wedges

Sriracha, for serving

1. Heat the oil in a medium heavy pot over medium heat until it shimmers. Stir in the mushrooms and cook, stirring occasionally, until the mushrooms are golden brown in spots, about 6 minutes. Stir in the ginger and garlic and cook until the garlic turns golden, about 2 minutes.

2. Add the stocks and bring to a boil; simmer for 10 minutes to intensify the broth. Add noodles and bok choy and let the broth come back to a boil. Season the shrimp with ½ to 1 teaspoon salt. Remove the pot from the heat and stir in the shrimp and soy sauce. Cover and let sit until the shrimp are cooked through, 2 to 3 minutes. Season with salt and pepper to taste. Top with sliced scallions and serve with lime and sriracha.

SLOW-ROASTED SALMON

WITH BARBECUE SAUCE AND SWISS CHARD

Quickly seared fish is great, but if you have a little extra time before dinner has to be on the table, try slow-roasting. It's a forgiving, stress-free method using a relatively low oven temp that leaves salmon moist with an especially buttery texture. That richness and the fish's big flavor just beg for something sweet and tangy, so I whip up a classic barbecue sauce to brush on while it's cooking. (Or use your favorite jarred version, especially if it's one of those without tons of sugar and unpronounceable ingredients.) While the sauce and salmon spend quality time in the oven, you can prep and cook a simple side of chard and tomatoes. Then, boom, you've got dinner.

SERVES 6 TO 8
Active time: 30 MINUTES
Start to finish: 1 HOUR

FOR THE BBQ SAUCE

1 tablespoon extra-virgin olive oil

1 small onion, chopped

1 small red bell pepper, stemmed, seeded, deveined, and chopped

3 garlic cloves, smashed

Kosher salt

1 tablespoon tomato paste

1 teaspoon ground cumin

1 pound ripe tomatoes, cored and coarsely chopped, or one 14.5-ounce can diced tomatoes

¼ cup apple cider vinegar

3 tablespoons honey or maple syrup

1. **MAKE THE BBQ SAUCE:** Heat the oil in a medium saucepan over medium-high heat until it shimmers. Add the onion, bell pepper, garlic, and 1 to 1½ teaspoons salt and cook, stirring occasionally, until the pepper is tender, 8 to 10 minutes. Stir in the tomato paste and cumin and cook, stirring frequently, until the tomato paste is a few shades darker, about 2 minutes. Stir in the tomatoes and cook until softened and thickened, about 8 minutes. Stir in the vinegar and honey, then transfer to a blender and puree until smooth. (Be careful when blending hot liquids; always secure the lid and protect your hand with a kitchen towel or oven mitt.) Season with more salt to taste.

The sauce keeps in an airtight container in the fridge for up to 2 weeks.

recipe continues

FOR THE SALMON AND SWISS CHARD

Six 6- to 8-ounce salmon fillets

Kosher salt

1 large bunch of Swiss chard, bottom ½ inch of stems trimmed

2 tablespoons extra-virgin olive oil

2 garlic cloves, thinly sliced

1 pint cherry tomatoes, halved

2. COOK THE SALMON AND CHARD: Preheat the oven to 325°F. Line a rimmed baking sheet with parchment paper.

3. Put the salmon on the lined baking sheet and lightly season with salt. Liberally brush the salmon with some of the BBQ sauce. Roast until it's just opaque in the center, 15 to 25 minutes, depending on the thickness of the fillets. Brush some more BBQ sauce onto the fish when it's done.

4. While the salmon cooks, coarsely chop the Swiss chard crosswise. Heat the oil in a large heavy skillet over medium heat until it shimmers. Stir in the Swiss chard, garlic, and ½ to 1 teaspoon of salt. Cook, stirring occasionally, until the stems are crisp-tender and the leaves are tender and silky, about 6 minutes. Stir in the cherry tomatoes and remove it from the heat. Season with more salt to taste.

5. Serve the salmon with the Swiss chard and extra BBQ sauce on the side.

"COME AS YOU ARE"
CA CRV

GRILLED SQUID

WITH CHARRED LEMONS AND HERBS

Squid's got it all. Because it reproduces quickly and prolifically, it's usually a sustainable choice and a good value. Because it's got a mild flavor, it plays well with others, from fish sauce and chiles to tomatoes and olives. The truth is, you barely have to do a thing to it—just a sprinkle of salt, high heat, a squeeze of lemon, and you're good—but here I have a little fun. I boost the flavor with a marinade so it cooks up extra tender, and toss grilled lemon slices, rind and all, into the salad for an intense hit of citrus. To clean squid, just pull the tentacles from the body, find and cut out the hard beak at the center of the tentacles, and pull out the quill from the body.

SERVES 4 TO 6
Active time: **30 MINUTES**
Start to finish: **1 HOUR**

2¼ pounds cleaned squid (bodies and tentacles)

1 lemon, cut into ¼-inch rounds, seeds flicked out

¼ cup packed fresh oregano sprigs

2 garlic cloves, smashed

3 tablespoons extra-virgin olive oil

Kosher salt and freshly ground black pepper

Grapeseed or vegetable oil, for the grill

Small handful of coarsely chopped fresh parsley

EQUIPMENT

Long wooden skewers, soaked in water for 30 minutes

1. In a large bowl, toss the squid with the lemon slices, oregano, garlic, olive oil, and 1 to 1½ teaspoons of salt. Let stand at room temperature for 30 minutes.

2. Preheat a gas or charcoal grill to high heat. Pour a little oil on a rag; grab the rag with tongs and rub the oil onto the grill grates to prevent sticking.

3. When the grill grates are very hot, grill the lemon slices until charred in spots, about 3 minutes, then transfer to the cutting board. Grill the squid just until it's opaque, turning once, 1 to 2 minutes total, then transfer to a cutting board. Cut the squid into bite-sized pieces and halve the lemon slices. Transfer the squid and lemon to a serving bowl and toss with the parsley and salt and pepper to taste.

GRILLED OCTOPUS

WITH LEMON-OLIVE SALAD

With practically every supermarket in America offering fish reduced to fillets on ice, it can be easy to forget that seafood comes from, you know, the sea. That's just one reason octopus is one of my favorite foods: When you fork a charred tentacle, it's clear you're about to dig into a creature from the deep. The other reasons are many. It's often sustainably caught—nabbed in pots and traps, rather than by trawls that drag along the ocean floor. It's easy to make at home. It has a texture like nothing else, super tender with a compelling chew. To amp up its mild flavor, I look to salty olives, parsley, and lemon, whether you simply squeeze the citrus on top or take the time to carve out segments for a thrilling blast of acidity in each bite.

You'll notice I suggest simmering the octopus with a wine cork. It's one of those old-school tricks for tenderizing the tough beast that probably doesn't actually have much of an effect. But I started doing it on the advice of Emilio Vitolo, my octopus guru and the chef behind the unpretentious, simple Italian food at Emilio's Ballato, in Manhattan. Whether adding the cork is good science or straight superstition, I'm not going to argue when the result is this good.

SERVES 6 TO 8
Active time: 25 MINUTES
Start to finish: 1½ HOURS

FOR SIMMERING THE OCTOPUS

One 4- to 5-pound fresh or thawed frozen cleaned octopus

1 garlic head, halved crosswise

1 lemon, halved

4 dried bay leaves

Kosher salt

1. **SIMMER THE OCTOPUS:** Cut the octopus head from the tentacles, then halve both the head and cluster of tentacles lengthwise. Locate the hole at the base where the tentacles all meet and use your fingers to push out the hard beak. Discard it. Rinse and drain the octopus and put it in a large pot along with the garlic, lemon halves, bay leaves, and enough water to cover the octopus by 2 inches or so. Add 3 tablespoons salt, or enough to make the water taste pleasantly salty. Add a wine cork, too, if you're superstitious. Bring to a boil over high heat, then cover and reduce the heat to maintain a moderate simmer and cook until you can easily insert a small sharp knife into the thick part of the tentacles, about 1 hour. Transfer the octopus to a cutting board and let it cool slightly.

recipe continues

FOR THE DISH

2 lemons

1 cup mixed pitted olives, coarsely chopped

Handful of roughly chopped fresh parsley

4 tablespoons extra-virgin olive oil

Kosher salt

Grapeseed or vegetable oil, for the grill

2. MAKE THE DISH: While the octopus is simmering, trim the tops and bottoms of the 2 lemons with a sharp knife. Then, working from top to bottom and following the curve of the fruit, carve off the peel and pith to expose the flesh. Cut each lemon segment from the membrane (don't stress about keeping each one intact) and drop it into a bowl. Coarsely chop the lemon segments, discarding any seeds, and add them to another bowl along with the olives, parsley, 2 tablespoons olive oil, and salt to taste. Toss well.

3. Preheat a gas or charcoal grill to high heat. Pour a little grapeseed or vegetable oil on a rag, grab the rag with tongs, and rub the oil onto the grill grates to prevent sticking.

4. Pat the octopus dry and toss with the remaining olive oil and lightly season with salt. When the grill grates are very hot, grill the octopus directly over the coals or flame, turning once, until lightly charred, about 10 minutes. Transfer to a cutting board. Cut the head into bite-sized pieces and leave the tentacles nice and long. Put it on a serving platter and top with the olive salad.

CIOPPINO

This soulful tomato-based seafood stew is a treat brought over by Italian immigrants and now an essential dish in my rotation. Cioppino is an excellent one-pot meal, overflowing with the taste of the sea, thanks to the flavor-fortifying qualities of anchovy paste and shellfish. It all adds up to the kind of broth that will have you reaching for an entire loaf's worth of grilled bread to sop it up—or since we're trying to eat better, maybe some whole-wheat couscous instead. Since any mild white-fleshed fish works, cioppino provides a great opportunity to let an ocean-friendly choice, like hake, pollack, or Pacific halibut, join the sustainable filter-feeders in the pot.

SERVES 6 TO 8
Active time: 40 MINUTES
Start to finish: 1¼ HOURS

- 2 tablespoons extra-virgin olive oil
- 1 large yellow onion, chopped
- 3 garlic cloves, thinly sliced
- Kosher salt
- 1 tablespoon anchovy paste
- ¼ teaspoon dried red pepper flakes
- 1 cup dry white wine
- Two 28-ounce cans whole tomatoes
- 2 cups fish stock or bottled clam juice
- 2 pounds shellfish, such as small clams or mussels, scrubbed well (see notes on pages 150 and 153)
- 1 pound lobster or shrimp (optional)
- 2 pounds skinless fillets of thick white-fleshed fish, such as hake, pollack, or halibut

1. Heat the oil in a large heavy pot over medium heat until it shimmers. Stir in the onion, garlic, and ½ teaspoon of salt and cook, stirring occasionally, until the onion is translucent, 5 to 6 minutes. Stir in the anchovy paste and pepper flakes and cook, stirring frequently, about 3 minutes. Stir in the wine and bring to a boil. Stir in the tomatoes with their juice and the stock and bring to a boil, breaking up the tomatoes with a wooden spoon. Reduce the heat, simmer until the flavors come together, about 30 minutes.

2. Add the shellfish and lobster (if using) and cook at a moderate simmer for 4 minutes. Stir in the fish and cook, stirring gently and occasionally, until the fish is cooked through and the shellfish have opened wide, about 4 minutes more. Remove the pot from heat. Season with salt to taste.

KILLING LOBSTER HUMANELY

If you're using live lobster, begin by putting it in the freezer for 15 minutes or so to dull its senses. Next, put the lobster belly-side down on a cutting board. Grab a chef's knife, position the tip at the back of the head, then quickly and with force, pierce the shell and bring the knife down between the eyes to split the head. Cut the body in half lengthwise, then twist off the claws. Use the back of a sturdy knife to whack and crack the knuckles and claws to help get to the meat.

SNEAKY ANCHOVY PASTA

FOR ALEX

My wife, Alex, had always hated anchovies. She is not alone. Preserved anchovies have an aggressively salty sea flavor that you either love or loathe. I'm in the love 'em camp. I eat them in all forms—in punchy sauces, draped over salads, piled on toast. But the magic of anchovies is that you don't have to like them to love what they can do. Because while Alex avoided food that showcased the fish, she adored my weeknight staple—spaghetti tossed with tomato, garlic, chiles, and (yep) anchovies.

When used with restraint and cooked in hot olive oil, anchovies almost literally melt into the background, transforming from fishy fillets into a subtle, nearly unidentifiable *something* that makes food taste better. Instead of dominating a dish, they can work behind the scenes to enhance its best qualities. With their help, that pasta goes from good to awesome, the already flavorful sauce bigger, bolder, and brighter. Since the anchovies don't announce themselves, a sly husband might even be tempted to keep their presence a secret. That would be short sighted. Alex is still not eating them straight from the can, but at least now can no longer say she doesn't like them.

SERVES 4 TO 6
Active time: 30 MINUTES
Start to finish: 30 MINUTES

2 tablespoons extra-virgin olive oil

2 large shallots or 1 small yellow onion, finely chopped

4 or 5 garlic cloves, thinly sliced

6 oil-packed anchovy fillets (or more to taste), finely chopped

Dried red pepper flakes, to taste

One 28-ounce can peeled whole tomatoes

Kosher salt

1 pound dried spaghetti or bucatini

Handful of fresh basil leaves

Big handful of finely grated Parmesan

1. Bring a large pot of well-salted water to a boil. Meanwhile, heat the olive oil in a large saucepan over medium-high heat until it shimmers. Add the shallots and garlic and cook, stirring frequently, until the garlic turns light golden, about 3 minutes.

2. Add the anchovies to the pan and cook, stirring occasionally, until they melt, about 2 minutes. Add a pinch or three of pepper flakes, stir well, and add the tomatoes. Bring the tomatoes to a simmer and cook, stirring occasionally and breaking them up with a wooden spoon, until the sauce thickens slightly, about 10 minutes. Season with salt, more pepper flakes, and more anchovy to taste and simmer for a couple minutes more.

3. Cook the pasta in the boiling water, stirring occasionally, until it's just a little less done than you'd like (it'll finish cooking as you finish the dish). Drain well, reserving about ¼ cup of the pasta water.

4. Add the pasta to the sauce and toss well with tongs, gradually adding pasta water as necessary to loosen the sauce. Divide among plates. Tear the basil leaves into large pieces and scatter them over the pasta, then sprinkle on the Parmesan.

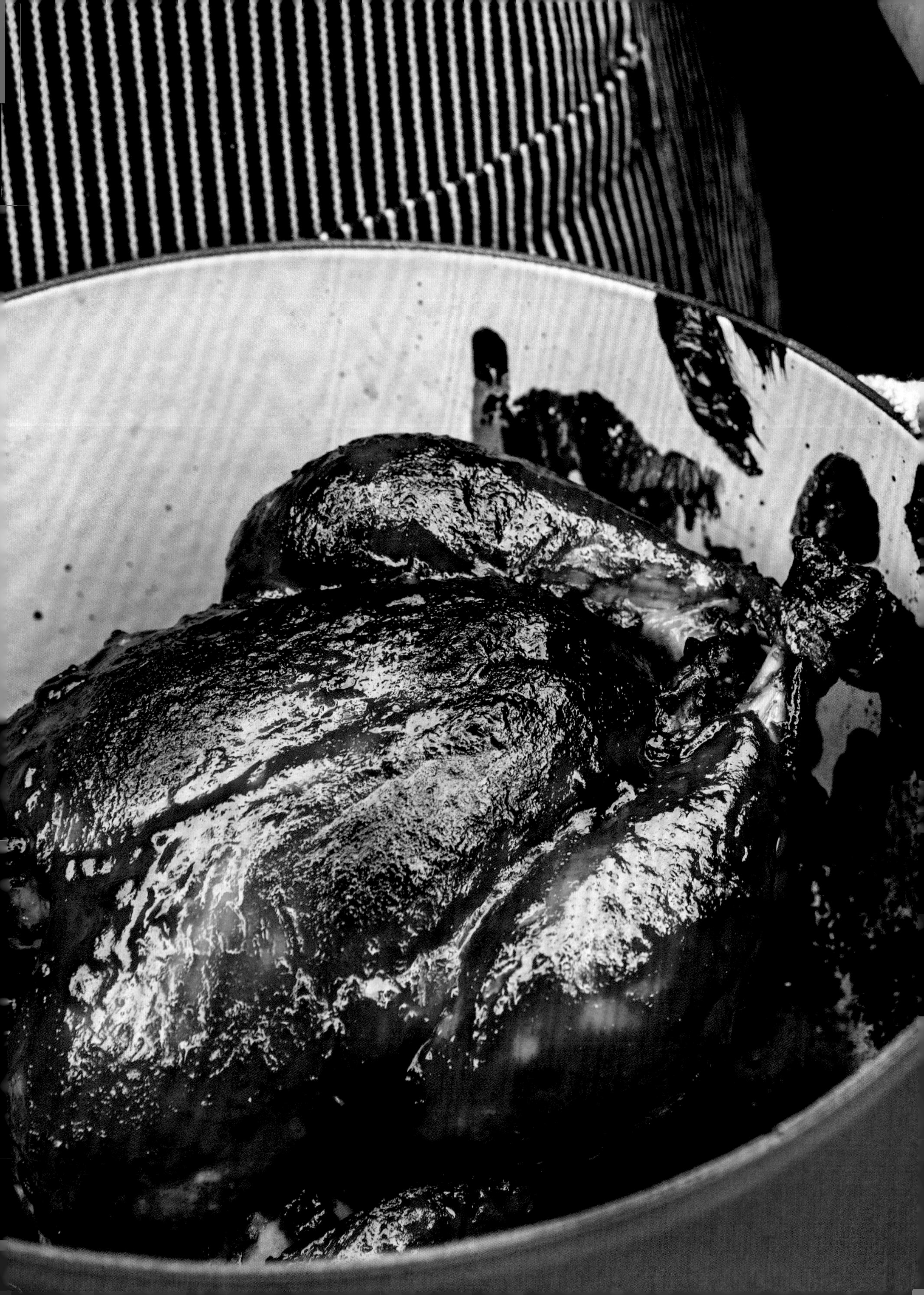

EAT
MORE
CHICKEN

DURING MY STINT in Vienna, I took a break to visit some friends in Piedmont, Italy. One night, they took me to a local family restaurant. After four hours of eating and drinking, we were all close to bursting, but the chef insisted on bringing us one last dish, what looked like rather plain poultry legs stewed in tomato sauce.

The meat had amazing flavor and texture. Maybe we were relishing some sort of guinea hen or a wild bird I'd never heard of. When the waiter came by, I sputtered a question that, in broken Italian, amounted to "What is this incredible creature I'm eating?" "*Pollo*," he replied, flatly. Chicken.

I count that as the moment I really tasted chicken for the first time. The reason I hadn't recognized it was that, up to that point, I had mainly eaten factory-farmed birds. What made this chicken taste so good, I soon learned, was that it had spent its days outside, roaming free, scratching at dirt, and pecking at bugs in grassy fields. In other words, the bird had lived well, doing and eating what it's meant to. Later, I learned that this type of husbandry has benefits beyond just the flavor of the meat. As the chickens do their thing, they're also tilling, fertilizing, and otherwise improving the soil. Healthy soil means less carbon dioxide in the atmosphere contributing to global warming. This realization blew my mind: I could eat the best-tasting chicken *and* have a positive impact on the environment. Food that's good for us and good for the environment does not have to represent some sort of sacrifice. Just the opposite. It often means eating *more* deliciously.

But since this book is about eating better, not eating perfect, let's get real. Not everyone can stomach the price of the chicken raised on the small farms that tend to employ the best, most humane practices. So how do you up your chicken game?

First, understand that every time you choose chicken instead of other meats, you're choosing the meat responsible for the lowest greenhouse gas emissions. On that front, we've already made progress—around 2010, chicken became the meat Americans eat most. So let's keep at it.

Second, free range or pasture-raised is best, but the other meaningful choice you can make is to buy antibiotic-free. For decades, this required a trip to a farmer's market or specialty shop. No longer. A combination of pressure from the medical community and a change in consumer demand has rocked the entire industry. In the past few years, America's three largest poultry producers—Perdue Farms, Tyson Foods, and Foster Farms—have either eliminated or significantly curtailed antibiotic usage on their birds, hundreds of millions per year. The issue here isn't about flavor or even animal welfare. Overuse of antibiotics creates antibiotic-resistant "superbugs," so this makes a drastic reduction in that risk.

THE BLUEPRINT

ROASTING CHICKEN

Roasting a bird whole is the easiest, cheapest, and tastiest way to make chicken. The approximate instructions are "add salt and put in oven." With little more than that, you get a home perfumed with rendered chicken fat, and pull from the oven a golden-brown, crisp-skinned, juicy argument for eating better.

All that for about half the price of boneless, skinless breasts. With the money you save, you could consider buying chicken that's been raised better—cage free is good, meaning the birds can go outside to a small area; pasture raised or free range is best—or buy two birds and roast them both at once. Then you've got food for the week (see page 178).

And lastly, don't be scared of undercooking chicken. Many people are, and end up overcooking it, losing its succulence. Take the bird's temperature earlier, rather than later; remember, you can always cook it more.

SERVES 4 TO 6
Active time: 15 MINUTES
Start to finish: 1 HOUR 15 MINUTES

Kosher salt
One 3½- to 4-pound chicken
1 tablespoon extra-virgin olive oil

1. Preheat the oven to 450°F and move a rack to the center position.

2. Sprinkle salt generously in the chicken cavity, then loosely tie the legs together with kitchen twine. Rub the oil all over the chicken and sprinkle it all over with 1 to 1½ teaspoons of salt. (To take the chicken to the next level, see the next page.)

3. Roast the chicken in a large heavy skillet or roasting pan until the skin is golden brown and cooked through, 50 to 60 minutes, rotating halfway through if you want, to help keep the browning even. To tell whether the chicken is cooked, give the thigh a poke with the tip of a knife—if the juices run clear, you're good. If you're finicky, insert a meat thermometer into the thickest part of the thigh (make sure it's not touching the bone). It's ready when the thermometer registers about 160°F. It'll creep up to 165°F as it rests.

4. Transfer the chicken to a cutting board. Cut off the tail and eat it—a reward for a job well done. Let the chicken rest for 10 minutes before you and your guests dig in.

THE NEXT LEVEL: For an even better bird, do what chefs do: Salt the chicken ahead of time—way ahead of time, at least 1 hour or up to 48 hours before you plan to cook (the longer the better). The salt finds its way into the flesh, giving you a more flavorful, succulent result. And if you leave the salted chicken uncovered in the fridge as it does its thing, the skin dries out, so it gets extra crisp in the oven.

COOK QUICKER: I roasted a lot of chicken at the White House. Early on, it was a relaxed affair. As the chicken browned in the oven, I'd chop vegetables or make some rice. Then the madness started. Suddenly, between Let's Move! initiatives and policy battles, I'd often get to the residence with barely enough time to tie on an apron. I needed every minute I could get. That's when I fell for spatchcocking. With just a few cuts, you can butterfly the chicken so it lies flat and, like magic, cooks more quickly and more evenly, plus more of the skin gets crispy. Here's how:

Stand the chicken up so that the drumsticks point toward the ceiling. Starting just next to the tail, tip your knife into the cavity and slice downward through the back; if your knife is positioned correctly, it should cut through the back pretty easily. Open the chicken up like a book and lay it down breast-side up. Make a small cut at the top of the breastbone, then, using your palm, gently but firmly flatten the chicken; you might hear a crack and it will lie flat. Season and roast at 450°F until golden brown and cooked through, 30 to 40 minutes.

VARIATIONS

LEMON-GARLIC-CAYENNE

Stir together 1 teaspoon finely grated lemon zest, 1 finely chopped garlic clove, and ½ teaspoon cayenne. Using your fingers, slip the mixture between the skin and breast meat. Salt the chicken cavity, then stuff in half a lemon and and tie the legs together. Season and roast as in the blueprint (page 173).

HERB-GARLIC

Mix 1 teaspoon finely chopped fresh thyme and/or rosemary leaves with 1 finely chopped garlic clove. Using your fingers, slip the mixture between the skin and breast meat. Season and roast as in the blueprint.

GINGER-SCALLION

Mix ¼ cup thinly sliced scallions with 1 tablespoon each finely chopped ginger and garlic. Using your fingers, slip the mixture between the skin and breast meat. Season and roast as in the blueprint.

BARBECUED CHICKEN

On the First Family's first night in the White House—the eve of Barack Obama's inauguration and just before he and his family rushed out to make appearances at the various celebrations around town—this is what they had for dinner. It was my first time cooking in the second-floor kitchen of the Residence. The pressure was on. Not because I needed to make an impression—I'd already been cooking for them for almost two years—but because that night, dinner had to serve as a comfort to four people whose lives were changing forever.

I don't know about you, but to me there are few things that put me at peace with the universe like the aroma of roasting chicken. And being from Chicago, both the First Family and I have saucy barbecue in our blood. So I brushed a sweet, tangy concoction on a whole bird and let the oven do the rest, the sauce concentrating in flavor as the Residence filled with the perfume of scalding sugar and hot chicken fat. As it cooked, I made brown rice and sautéed broccoli with garlic. Soon, the family appeared and ate quickly before racing to join the festivities, the chicken picked clean—and the broccoli and rice gone, too.

SERVES 4 TO 6
Active time: **10 MINUTES**
Start to finish: **1¼ HOURS**

½ cup ketchup
¼ cup molasses (not blackstrap)
2 tablespoons apple cider vinegar
1 tablespoon Worcestershire sauce
1 tablespoon sriracha
Kosher salt
One 3½- to 4-pound chicken

1. Preheat the oven to 450°F.

2. Stir together the ketchup, molasses, vinegar, Worcestershire, Sriracha, and ½ teaspoon of salt, or to taste.

3. Put the chicken in a large heavy ovenproof skillet or roasting pan. Season inside and out with salt and brush some of the sauce generously all over the top and sides of chicken. Roast, occasionally brushing with additional sauce and rotating the skillet to help keep the browning even, until it's deep brown, charred in spots, and cooked through, about 60 minutes.

4. Transfer the chicken to a cutting board. Let the chicken rest for 10 minutes before you dig in.

LEFTOVER CHICKEN

With a roasted chicken, the party doesn't end when dinner does. After the plates are cleared, I get in there with my fingers, hunting for any meat and skin left on the bones. Once I'm done, I have a heap of chicken—and some of the best bits at that—to make an easy lunch or dinner the next day. And don't forget about the carcass, which I use to boost store-bought broth or slip into a freezer bag for future use. Once you save up three or four, you've got the key to a killer stock.

ROASTED CHICKEN STIR-FRY

Leftover chicken transforms a simple vegetable stir-fry from side dish into dinner. Nothing fancy here. Just crisp-tender broccoli, lots of scallions, and meaty shiitake mushrooms, which bring on the umami—you know, that elusive flavor that makes food taste extra good. And again, feel free to sub in about a pound of any vegetables you have for the broccoli: cauliflower, green beans, asparagus, any leafy greens. Or firmer stuff like carrots, turnips, and the like; just slice those into thin pieces so they cook through.

SERVES 4 TO 6
Active time: 30 MINUTES
Start to finish: 30 MINUTES

3 tablespoons vegetable oil

6 ounces small shiitake mushrooms, stems removed, sliced

1 head of broccoli, cut into bite-sized florets and peeled stem pieces

1 bunch scallions, roots trimmed, thinly sliced

2 tablespoons peeled and finely chopped fresh ginger

3 garlic cloves, finely chopped

Kosher salt

2 cups shredded cooked chicken (ideally, meat *and* skin)

2 tablespoons soy sauce

Toasted sesame oil to taste

1. Heat the oil in a large heavy skillet over high heat until it shimmers, add the mushrooms in a more or less single layer, and cook, without stirring, until they're golden brown, about 4 minutes. Add the broccoli, scallions, ginger, garlic, and a generous ½ teaspoon of salt and cook, stirring occasionally, until the broccoli and garlic get a little color, 2 to 3 minutes more.

2. Add ¼ cup of water, cover, and cook just until the broccoli turns bright green and is crisp-tender, about 2 minutes. Uncover, add the chicken, and cook, stirring occasionally, until all the water has evaporated and the chicken is heated through, about 2 minutes. Take the skillet off the heat and stir in the soy sauce and up to 1 tablespoon sesame oil. Season with salt to taste.

CHICKEN SALAD

To stretch last night's chicken into today's lunch, I turn to this back-pocket classic. A healthy splash of vinegar and fresh thyme amp up the typical mayo-focused mixture. Then I lean on whatever I've got on hand to add extra texture and flavor. Here, I swap raw green beans for the usual celery and add red onion for extra crunch and a little sweetness, but you should use whatever crisp, fresh elements you have available: diced radishes, apple, kohlrabi, cabbage, and so on.

SERVES 4 TO 6
Active time: 15 MINUTES
Start to finish: 15 MINUTES

2 cups shredded cooked chicken (ideally, meat *and* skin)
1 cup thinly sliced raw green beans
¼ cup finely chopped red onion
⅓ cup mayo (or olive oil and vinegar to taste)
1 to 2 tablespoons champagne or white wine vinegar
1 teaspoon finely chopped fresh thyme leaves
Kosher salt

Toss the chicken together with the beans, onion, mayonnaise, 1 tablespoon vinegar, thyme, and ¼ to ½ teaspoon of salt. Season with more vinegar and salt to taste.

SOUPED-UP CHICKEN STOCK

Once you have a bunch of chicken carcasses saved up, it's time to make stock. But when you just have one, you can still put it to great use. I brown it in a little butter to coax out as much flavor as possible, then simmer it with some aromatics (vegetables or herbs) in store-bought stock. Suddenly, the tame boxed stuff morphs into a supercharged liquid that improves virtually anything it touches—whether you sub it for water when you cook grains or add a splash to your next stir-fry. Freeze it in ice cube trays, then transfer the cubes to freezer bags so you can use as much (or as little) as you like.

MAKES ABOUT 7 CUPS
Active time: 15 MINUTES
Start to finish: 45 MINUTES

1 roasted-chicken carcass
1 tablespoon unsalted butter
1 carrot, chopped
1 celery stalk, chopped
1 shallot, halved
2 quarts store-bought low-sodium chicken stock

1. Use your hands to break the carcass into 8 or so pieces. Heat the butter in a large heavy pot over medium heat until it melts and froths, then add the chicken carcass, carrot, celery, and shallot. Cook, stirring only once or twice, until the carcass is golden in places, about 6 minutes. Add the stock, bring to a simmer, and cook at a gentle simmer for 30 minutes.

2. Strain the liquid, discarding the solids. Use right away or let cool and refrigerate in an airtight container for up to 1 week or freeze for up to 6 months.

SAUTÉED CHICKEN LIVERS

If chicken livers have a bad rap, it's because they're so often overcooked. But if you take care to keep the insides still slightly pink, their creamy texture can convert even the most committed abstainers. The delicate flavor of chicken livers helps, too, as does a generous dollop of crème fraîche. A squeeze of lemon yanks it all back from the brink of being too rich. Toss them with buttered egg noodles (think beef stroganoff, but better) or spoon them over rice or garlic-rubbed grilled toasts.

SERVES 4 TO 6
Active time: 20 MINUTES
Start to finish: 20 MINUTES

1¼ pounds chicken livers, rinsed

2 tablespoons unsalted butter

Kosher salt

1 large onion, finely chopped

2 garlic cloves, peeled and smashed

½ cup crème fraîche or sour cream

Big handful chopped parsley or a few tablespoons finely chopped fresh herbs, such as rosemary, sage, and/or thyme

½ lemon

Freshly ground black pepper

1. Pat the livers very dry with paper towels. Heat the butter in a large, heavy skillet over high heat and let it froth. Season the livers generously with salt and add them to the pan. Cook, flipping once, until browned on both sides but still pink in the center, 3 to 4 minutes.

2. Transfer the livers to a plate with a slotted spoon. Lower the heat to medium and add the onion, garlic, and a generous pinch of salt to the pan. Cook, stirring and scraping up the browned bits, until the onion is soft and golden, about 10 minutes. Stir the livers back into the pan (along with any juices) to reheat them.

3. Remove the pan from the heat and stir in the crème fraiche and herbs. Squeeze the lemon over and season with salt and pepper to taste.

DIRTY BROWN RICE

A sort of rice pilaf, this dish combines rice with chicken liver, flecking the grains with brown and giving them a dirty look, not to mention an awesome flavor that even liver skeptics will love. My version is even "dirtier" than the Louisiana Creole classic, because I double down on the color and use brown rice, which might make purists wince but is even tastier, in a nutty, chewier way.

SERVES 4 TO 6
Active time: **20 MINUTES**
Start to finish: **1 HOUR**

1½ cups short-grain brown rice
Kosher salt
½ pound chicken livers
2 tablespoons unsalted butter
1 medium onion, finely chopped
¼ teaspoon cayenne pepper
1 bunch of scallions, roots trimmed and thinly sliced

1. Combine the rice and 1 quart water in a medium pot with ½ teaspoon of salt. Bring to a boil over high heat, reduce the heat to low, cover, and cook until the grains are tender but still slightly chewy, about 40 minutes. Drain the rice in a colander, transfer to a large serving bowl, and cover to keep warm.

2. While the rice is cooking, rinse the livers under running water, pat them very dry with paper towels, and season generously with salt.

3. Melt the butter in a large heavy skillet over medium-high heat, then stir in the onion and ½ teaspoon of salt. Cook, stirring occasionally, until the onion is translucent, about 3 minutes. Stir in the chicken livers and cayenne and cook, stirring occasionally, until the livers are browned on the outside and still slightly pink in the center, about 6 minutes. Scoop the livers onto a cutting board, coarsely chop them, and add them and the contents of the skillet to the bowl with the rice. Add the scallions, ½ teaspoon salt, and stir well. Season with more salt to taste.

POTUS'S LUCKY PASTA

Even if you weren't following politics during the 2012 election, you probably heard about the first presidential debate. The president faced off against former Massachusetts governor Mitt Romney in Denver, and let's just say it didn't go as planned. One of President Obama's weaknesses, as he readily admits, was his impatience with the show of politics. In that debate, he delivered a sober, detailed discussion of policy. And he paid the price. His performance was universally panned in the media and Governor Romney's poll numbers surged. The pundits declared that if Obama tanked another debate, he would probably lose the election. Needless to say, the pressure was on.

I was on food and hangout duty during debate season, traveling with the president and helping to feed him in the run-up to all three. After the unfortunate first contest, his staff spent three days holed up at a hotel in Virginia as he battled through grueling practice sessions. Practically the only breaks he took were to eat. Finally, the day of the second debate arrived. The plan was to head to Hofstra University, on Long Island, around lunchtime. By late morning, I still hadn't gotten word on whether the president, who'd eaten a late breakfast, would want food on the plane ride, so just in case, I started cooking. In the hotel kitchen, I prepped and packed the makings of a simple lunch: I cooked a chicken breast, whipped up a classic pesto, and boiled mini penne just shy of al dente. I grabbed some raw spinach and Parmesan, then loaded into the motorcade with the rest of the president's staff, all of us wearing our best "We're totally relaxed and confident" faces, but all of us nervous.

When Air Force One took off, I stopped by the plane's conference room to see if the president wanted something to eat. In the middle of a game of Spades, he hemmed and hawed a bit, then said, "Sure, just nothing too heavy." I had my marching orders, so off I went to the kitchen to prepare the first and only meal I cooked on the president's plane.

The kitchen on Air Force One is surprisingly tiny and intimidatingly immaculate. When I got there, it was crammed with the two Air Force chefs prepping to serve lunch to the hundred-plus people—including White House staff, Secret Service, and press—onboard. They stopped work when they spotted me, as they did whenever the boss needed to eat. I wedged my way in, turned on one of the four induction burners, and got to work. I resuscitated the penne in a pan with a little olive oil and water, tossed in the chicken, and then the spinach. I hit it with some pesto, trying my best to avoid defiling the pristine stove with green spatter, threw on a handful of grated Parm, and hustled a plate to the president, who was both deep in Spades mode and reviewing a stack of papers.

After a few minutes, I popped back in to see if he was happy, assuming I'd get a simple "solid." Instead, he beamed at me. "Sam, it's perfect!" he raved. "Sometimes you don't know what you want until someone gives it to you, and you realize, 'That's exactly what I wanted.'"

I had never seen him react quite like that to anything I'd cooked. After he'd finished, I returned to hang out and he delivered another round of praise for the pasta. Later, just before he took the stage at Hofstra, I bumped into my friend Pete Souza, the president's photographer, who told me, "I don't know what you put in the pasta but the president has been talking about it all afternoon."

He did well that night, dominating the debate and making his case to the American people with clarity and passion. He shifted the election's momentum and all of us in the administration had a rare restful night's sleep. Before I turned in, I sent him an email: "It doesn't get better than that! One more left." He replied with one line: "It was the pasta!"

From then on, it became known as "Lucky Pasta." I made it for him again before the third and final debate, and he turned in a stellar performance—no thanks I'm sure to rigorous prep and a firm command of the subjects of foreign policy and national security. Come on, it was the pasta! Because I'll tell you what: I also made it on Election Day.

LUCKY PASTA

You may not have an election or debate coming up, but we all need a lucky charm, or at least a meal that comes together in minutes. Feel free to cook the chicken, boil the pasta, and even make the pesto the night before. If you do, undercook the pasta slightly or reheat it in just a little water in a saute pan. Store the pesto in the fridge with plastic wrap pressed against the surface to keep natural discoloration at a minimum.

SERVES 4 TO 6
Active time: **20 MINUTES**
Start to finish: **20 MINUTES**

1 pound mini penne or any pasta shape you like

Kosher salt

½ garlic clove

2 cups packed fresh basil leaves

¼ cup pine nuts or pecans, toasted

⅓ cup finely grated Parmesan cheese, plus more to finish

½ cup extra-virgin olive oil

2 cooked chicken breasts (see below), cut into bite-sized pieces, warm or room temperature

½ pound baby spinach

1. Cook the pasta in boiling salty water until al dente. Drain, reserving 1 cup of the water.

2. While the pasta cooks, drop the garlic into a food processor with the motor running and process until the garlic is finely chopped. Add the basil, nuts, cheese, half the oil, and ½ teaspoon of salt and pulse to a coarse puree. With the motor running, add the remaining oil in a slow stream and keep processing until pretty smooth.

3. Toss the hot pasta with the pesto, chicken, spinach, and ⅓ cup of the reserved pasta water. Gradually add more of the pasta water if the dish seems dry. Season with salt to taste and top with more grated or shaved parmesan.

Simply Roasted Chicken Breasts

2 skin-on chicken breasts, about 6 ounces each

1 tablespoon extra-virgin olive oil

Kosher salt

Preheat the oven to 450°F. Put the chicken breasts on a parchment-lined baking sheet and coat with the oil. Season generously all over with salt, about 1 teaspoon total. Roast them skin-side up until lightly browned and fully cooked but still juicy, about 20 minutes. Let them rest on a cutting board for a few minutes, then cut into bite-sized pieces.

BRAISED CHICKEN

WITH ORANGE AND OLIVES

Anyone who thinks chicken is dull has to try this braise. Olives and oranges, which you see together in Sicilian and Moroccan cooking, form one of those unions that only seems unexpected until your first bite.

SERVES 4 TO 6
Active time: 30 MINUTES
Start to finish: 1 HOUR

1 tablespoon vegetable oil
4 chicken legs (about 2 pounds)
Kosher salt
1 large onion, chopped
1½ cups low-sodium chicken stock
1 cup pitted green olives, roughly chopped
3 long, wide strips orange zest, white pith cut away
½ cup fresh orange juice
1 tablespoon dried juniper berries (optional)
1 fresh thyme sprig or ½ teaspoon dried thyme

1. Preheat the oven to 350°F and position an oven rack in the upper third. Heat the oil in a large heavy skillet over medium heat until it shimmers. Pat the chicken dry with paper towels, then season generously with salt. Cook the chicken skin-side down, without messing with it much, until the skin is golden brown, 8 to 10 minutes. Flip and brown the other side, about 3 minutes. Transfer the chicken to a plate.

2. Add the onion to the pan, occasionally stirring and scraping up any browned bits, and cook until golden at the edges, about 8 minutes. Add the stock, olives, orange zest, orange juice, juniper berries (if using), and thyme. Return the chicken to the pan, skin-side up, along with any juices left on the plate. (Ideally the liquid will come about halfway up the sides of the chicken, but don't sweat it if not.) Bring the liquid to a simmer and then roast in the oven, uncovered, until the chicken is tender and the skin is brown and crisp, about 45 minutes. I like to broil it for the last few minutes to get the skin extra crispy.

3. Season the sauce with salt to taste, though it may not need any.

BRAISE THAT CHICKEN

I hope my braised chicken gets you hooked on the thrilling combo of olives and oranges. I also hope it opens up a door. Because whenever you find yourself with bone-in dark meat chicken, you can braise it, and as long you follow the general formula, you're going to be very happy no matter what flavor profile you settle on. While most braises instruct you to cover the pan, my preferred way to do it is to place the chicken skin-side up in the liquid and cook it in the oven to give you a concentrated sauce and crisp skin. Here's how:

1. Heat a generous splash of oil in a wide, heavy pan with a lid. Brown generously salted chicken on both sides, then transfer it to a plate, leaving the chicken-infused fat behind.

2. Cook aromatics (chopped garlic, onions, ginger, carrots, celery, fennel, etc.) in the fat.

3. Pour in a flavorful liquid (stock, or a mixture of soy sauce and rice vinegar, or beer, you name it), scrape up all the browned bits in the pan, add some herbs or spices, and return the chicken skin-side up to the pan; ideally, the liquid will come about halfway up the sides of the chicken.

4. Roast, uncovered, until the meat twists off easily with a fork and the skin is deep brown and crisp, about 45 minutes. I like to broil it for the last few minutes to get the skin extra crispy.

5. Taste the liquid in the pan. If it tastes nice and rich, gradually add salt and lemon or vinegar until you like what you've got. If it doesn't taste rich enough, take out the chicken, turn up the heat, and let the liquid bubble away until it concentrates in flavor, then season until it tastes awesome. Serve with any simply cooked whole grain.

GRILLED CHICKEN THIGHS

WITH POMEGRANATE AND THYME

Eating better does not mean a life sentence of boneless, skinless chicken breasts. Choose thighs and you're already guaranteed more flavorful, juicy meat, and that's before you hit them with a glaze made from orange juice, zest, fresh thyme, and pomegranate molasses. Available at Middle Eastern grocers and many markets, each bottle contains your new favorite pantry ingredient, the juice of the pomegranate reduced to an intensely tart, slightly sweet syrup. Once you've got it, flaunt it: Drizzle it anywhere you'd think to use balsamic—into dressings, over sweet roasted vegetables, on grilled or roasted meats.

SERVES 4 TO 6
Active time: 30 MINUTES
Start to finish: 35 MINUTES

Grapeseed or vegetable oil, for the grill

⅓ cup pomegranate molasses

1 teaspoon finely grated orange zest

3 tablespoons fresh orange juice

1 teaspoon chopped fresh thyme leaves

Kosher salt

2 pounds skin-on, bone-in chicken thighs

1. Preheat a gas or charcoal grill so you have areas of medium heat and low heat. Pour a little oil on a rag; grab the rag with tongs and rub the oil onto the grill grates to prevent sticking.

2. Meanwhile, stir together the pomegranate molasses, orange zest, orange juice, thyme, and a generous pinch of salt. Pour about half of the glaze into a small bowl.

3. When the grill's ready, lightly season the thighs all over with salt. Grill over medium heat, flipping occasionally and moving them to the low-heat area if they threaten to get too dark, until browned and almost cooked through, 20 to 25 minutes. Brush the thighs with half of the glaze, then keep grilling until the chicken is cooked through, about 5 minutes more. Transfer to a serving platter and drizzle with the remaining glaze.

BRINE FOR BETTER BONELESS, SKINLESS

Whether you've got whole chicken parts or boneless, skinless breasts, take them to the next level by brining them overnight. A brine—salty water, at its most basic—infuses the meat with flavor and makes each bite taste extra juicy and delicious, so I especially like to do it when I've got meat without flavor-giving bone and skin and have time to plan ahead. This brine works for pork, too, and you can add any herb or spice you like.

MAKES 1 QUART, ENOUGH FOR 2 POUNDS CHICKEN (IT'S EASILY DOUBLED)

1 quart warm water

2 tablespoons maple syrup or brown sugar

2 garlic cloves, smashed

1 onion, quartered

3 bay leaves

¼ cup kosher salt

In a large bowl, combine the water, maple syrup, garlic, onion, bay leaves, and salt, stirring until the salt dissolves. Let the brine cool to room temperature. Put the chicken in a deep bowl or a large resealable bag and pour in the brine. Cover or seal and refrigerate overnight. When ready to cook, drain the chicken and pat it dry. Since your chicken is now seasoned, you can skip seasoning with salt before cooking.

A LITTLE
PORK
IS ALL
GOOD
au Château
2714

ANYONE WORRIED that eating better means eating bland must meet the pork shoulder. It enters the oven a hunk of muscle and fat and leaves a golden brown, glistening spectacle with meat so tender that it comes off with a nudge from a spoon, as versatile as it is delicious. Anyone concerned that they can't quit steaks and burgers should inhale over a pair of pork chops caramelizing in a pan as they send up the nothing-like-it-on-earth aroma of their melting fat. It only seems too good to be true: This really is what eating better can look like.

When you pile that ridiculously tender shoulder on your plate or cut juicy slices off those chops, you don't have to think about pork's significantly smaller carbon footprint—when it's raised right, pork can be part of a healthy agricultural system; even when it's not, it's still better than beef.

Don't get me wrong: Pork isn't really health food. I don't advise taking down a one-pound chop on your own. But its big, rich flavor even serves as a check on portion size, making the task of cutting down our typical monster protein portions easier than it is with, say, chicken—you just don't need that much of pork's fabulously fatty meat to feel satisfied. And if you or anyone you're feeding is skeptical about eating vegetables or whole grains, a bit of pork makes a great ambassador.

THE BLUEPRINT

ROASTED PORK SHOULDER

It doesn't get much better than slow-roasted pork shoulder's rich, flavor-packed meat. And since one shoulder is enough for a small army, it keeps the game going all week, as you can mix and match it with different vegetables and grains.

At its simplest, cooking the shoulder requires nothing more than salt and perhaps some stock or white wine to help loosen the tasty stuff that gets stuck to the pan and turn it into a kind of gravy. But I also provide three tweaks to take the dish in different directions. Whatever you choose, the shoulder does the heavy lifting, basting itself with its own fat and its meat transforming from tough to tender through the magic of slow cooking.

SERVES 10 TO 12
Active time: 30 MINUTES
Start to finish: 5 TO 48 HOURS (IF BRINING)

One 5- to 6-pound bone-in pork shoulder (sometimes called Boston butt)

Kosher salt

1 cup low-sodium chicken stock or dry white wine

1. Rub the pork all over with 1 tablespoon of salt. Let sit at room temperature for up to 2 hours (the longer the better). Or, brine it. (See page 199.)

2. Preheat the oven to 300°F.

3. Put the pork shoulder fat-side up on a heavy roasting pan (you can line it with foil, or parchment paper, which I prefer) and stick it in the oven. Roast, peering in to ogle occasionally, until the meat is deep golden brown and so tender it's practically falling apart, about 5 hours. (But check at 4.) For a little more color, broil the shoulder for a few minutes to finish it off and to crisp the meat.

4. Turn off the heat and take the pan out of the oven. Carefully transfer the shoulder to a serving plate. Pour the stock or wine into the pan, and set it over medium heat, and as it bubbles, use a wooden spoon to scrape up any browned bits. Let the pork stand for 15 minutes at room temperature before serving with the pan liquid on top.

VARIATIONS

ROSEMARY, GARLIC, AND CAYENNE

I can't get enough of the combo of garlic and rosemary, plus a little cayenne for kick.

5 large garlic cloves, finely chopped

Kosher salt

2 tablespoons finely chopped fresh rosemary leaves

¼ to ½ teaspoon cayenne pepper

Use the flat side of a chef's knife to mince, mash, and scrape the garlic and ½ teaspoon of salt to a paste. Mix the paste with the rosemary and cayenne, and rub the mixture all over the seasoned pork, then continue with the recipe on page 197.

ONION-GRAINY MUSTARD

In this version, you roast the shoulder on a bed of mustardy onions. By the time the shoulder is tender, the onions underneath have soaked up the pork juices and turned sweet and jammy. Whole-grain mustard delivers a little bite and acidity.

3 large onions, cut into ¾-inch slices

⅓ cup grainy mustard

Combine the onions and mustard in the roasting pan and stir well. Set the seasoned pork on top of the onions and roast, continuing with the recipe on page 197. Check occasionally; if the onions are browning too quickly, splash some water or stock into the pan. Serve the onions and juices with the pork.

SHALLOTS WITH APPLE CIDER

Shallots catch the drippings from that big hunk of meat, turning porky and sweet, and then commune with cider to make the best sauce.

1½ cups apple cider

8 large shallots, peeled

Pour the cider into the roasting pan with the seasoned pork, add the shallots around the pork, then continue the recipe on page 197. Check occasionally; if the shallots are browning too quickly, add some stock or water to the pan. Mash the cooked shallots with a fork and serve with the pork.

PORK BRINE

Once you start brining, you'll never go back. Whether you're cooking a gigantic pork shoulder or a small chop, this method gives you the juiciest, tastiest meat every time.

MAKES 2 QUARTS ENOUGH FOR 6 POUNDS PORK

½ cup maple syrup or brown sugar

2 garlic cloves, smashed and peeled

2 dried bay leaves

2 small dried red chiles

Kosher salt

Bring 2 quarts water, the maple syrup, garlic, bay leaves, chiles, and 6 tablespoons salt to a simmer in a large pot, stirring to dissolve the salt. Cool completely. Submerge chops and brine in the fridge 4 to 12 hours and shoulders for 12 to 48 hours, then drain and thoroughly pat the meat dry. If you brine, there's no need to season with salt before cooking.

BEER-BRAISED PORK SHOULDER

WITH CARAWAY AND GARLIC

While roasting is a go-to method for shoulder, whenever I want saucier meat that's falling-apart tender, I add a little more liquid and cook it covered—in other words, I braise it. This version is Austrian to the core. I did my formative culinary training in a fancy restaurant in Vienna, where many of the dishes were high-end versions of country cooking. When I left, I found I craved not the fussy food but its soulful inspiration, like this beer-spiked braise fueled by the classic combo of pork, caraway seeds, and garlic. I watched cooks there take the garlic to the brink of burnt, so it provides extra complexity and rich color. Yet just like my braised chicken (page 190), this particular recipe provides a blueprint for your own take on succulent shoulder. Just follow the steps—sautéing aromatics, pouring in tasty liquid and spices or herbs, then adding a seasoned hunk of shoulder. As long as you cover tightly and cook slow, you'll be eating well.

SERVES 8 TO 10
Active time: 30 MINUTES
Start to finish: 5¾ HOURS

1 tablespoon vegetable oil

1 head of garlic, halved crosswise

2 large onions, coarsely chopped

Kosher salt

Two 12-ounce bottles mild beer

1 cup low-sodium chicken stock

1 tablespoon caraway seeds

One 5- to 6-pound bone-in pork shoulder (sometimes called Boston butt)

1. Preheat the oven to 350°F.

2. Heat the oil in a medium heavy skillet over medium-high heat until it shimmers. Add the garlic, cut-sides down, and cook until it's very dark brown and basically burnt, about 7 minutes. Stir in the onions and a few pinches of salt and cook, stirring occasionally, until the onions turn translucent, about 10 minutes.

3. Transfer the mixture to a heavy roasting pan and pour 1 bottle of the beer into the skillet, scraping up any browned bits. Pour the liquid into the roasting pan and add the remaining beer, stock, and the caraway seeds.

4. Rub the pork all over with 1½ tablespoons of salt and add it fat-side up to the roasting pan. Cover the roasting pan with parchment paper, then foil, and roast for 4 hours. Remove the parchment paper and foil and continue to roast until the meat is practically falling apart and the fat on top of the shoulder is crispy, about 1 hour more. (I like to flash it under the broiler for more color and crispness.) Remove the pan from the oven and let the pork rest for about 20 minutes. Season with salt to taste and serve.

LEFTOVER PORK SHOULDER

Since pork improves almost anything, I use leftover shoulder to make the good-for-you stuff more enticing. When you brown it in a hot pan, even a judicious portion ensures that your toughest customers—broccoli skeptics, white-rice fanatics—are excited for their plates, filled out with simple roasted vegetables and cooked grains.

RIGATONI WITH PORK RAGU

Classic ragu cooks for ages. But because you've already slow-roasted shoulder, this version takes a fraction of the time and still delivers the same pleasures—tender meat and porky juices that meld with tomatoes for a sauce that could make even whole-wheat pasta feel like a treat. If you like heat, dried red pepper flakes are great here.

SERVES 4 TO 6
Active time: 25 MINUTES
Start to finish: 35 TO 60 MINUTES

3 tablespoons extra-virgin olive oil

1 medium yellow onion, finely chopped

3 garlic cloves, smashed

Kosher salt

3 pounds ripe tomatoes, cored and chopped, or one 28-ounce can tomatoes in juice

2 to 3 cups coarsely shredded cooked pork shoulder (pages 197–201)

1 pound rigatoni

Big handful of grated Parmesan cheese

1. Heat the oil in a large heavy pot over medium-high heat until it shimmers. Stir in the onion, garlic, and ½ teaspoon of salt and cook, stirring occasionally, until the onion turns golden, about 8 minutes. Stir in the tomatoes and pork, let the mixture come to a simmer, and cook, breaking up the tomatoes, until you have a thick, rich sauce, about 25 minutes for fresh tomatoes or 15 minutes for canned. Season with salt to taste.

2. Meanwhile, cook the rigatoni in a large pot of salty boiling water until al dente. Drain well, toss with the sauce, and sprinkle on the Parm.

WHITE BEAN, PORK, AND GREENS SOUP

Without the pork, I'd eat this soup every other day. With it, I'd have it every night. It's a great way to use simply cooked grains, like farro (page 240) or bulgur (page 252), and any greens you have hanging around in the fridge. Just a 10-minute simmer with that left-over pork transforms store-bought stock into a broth that tastes homemade.

SERVES 4 TO 6
Active time: 20 MINUTES
Start to finish: 30 MINUTES

2 tablespoons extra-virgin olive oil

2 garlic cloves, thinly sliced

5 cups low-sodium chicken stock

One 15-ounce can low-sodium Great Northern or other white beans with their liquid

2 to 3 cups coarsely shredded cooked pork shoulder (pages 197–201)

1 bunch of mustard greens or Swiss chard, stem bottoms trimmed, torn or cut into bite-sized pieces

1 to 2 cups cooked grains, such as farro or bulgur (optional)

Kosher salt

1. Heat the oil in a medium heavy pot over medium heat until it shimmers. Stir in the garlic and cook, stirring, until it turns golden, about 2 minutes; then stir in the stock, beans along with their liquid, pork, and greens.

2. Raise the heat to bring it to a boil, then reduce the heat and simmer until the greens are tender, about 10 minutes. Stir in the grains (if using) and cook just until the soup comes back to a simmer. Season with salt to taste.

WARM BARLEY SALAD

WITH PORK, CHERRY TOMATOES, AND BASIL

As I got older, barley went from being the punchline in the joke of healthy dinner to a chewy, nutty treat I crave. Like all foods, it just needs salt, fat, and acid to come alive. Here, rich chunks of pork, vinegar, and tomatoes provide just that, while sweet onions and a blast of basil raise the deliciousness bar higher. If you have the time and inclination, choose hulled barley, which has more good stuff than the quicker-cooking pearl barley. Of course, any cooked grain like brown rice, bulgur, or quinoa would work here as well.

SERVES 4 TO 6
Active time: **25 MINUTES**
Start to finish: **2 HOURS**

Kosher salt

1½ cups hulled barley, rinsed

3 tablespoons extra-virgin olive oil

1 medium red onion, finely chopped

2 to 3 cups coarsely chopped cooked pork shoulder (pages 197–201)

1 pint cherry tomatoes, halved

2 tablespoons sherry or red wine vinegar, plus more to taste

Big handful fresh basil leaves

1. Bring a large pot of water to a boil, add salt so the water tastes slightly salty, and stir in the barley. Reduce the heat to maintain a steady simmer and cook, stirring occasionally, until it's tender but still pleasantly chewy, about 1 hour. Drain it in a strainer.

2. Heat 2 tablespoons of the oil in a Dutch oven or medium heavy pot over medium-high heat until it shimmers. Add the onion and a generous pinch of salt and cook, stirring, until soft and lightly browned, about 12 minutes.

3. Add the pork and cook, stirring occasionally, until hot, about 5 minutes more. Stir in the drained barley, tomatoes, and vinegar and cook just until it's all warm, a few minutes. Remove it from the heat, stir in the remaining 1 tablespoon oil, season with salt and more vinegar. Tear the basil leaves and stir them in. Serve warm.

BRAISED PORK CHEEKS

WITH SAUERKRAUT AND PEAR

Once you try pork cheeks, you're hooked. With some long, gentle cooking, these nuggets take on the most luscious texture, which can put even shoulder to shame. A good butcher might stock them—if they're not in the cold case, try begging. (If that fails, settle for another cut that takes well to slow cooking, like blade steaks, meaty cuts of belly, or shoulder.) And when you do score, prepare them like this, braised with sauerkraut and pears; the cooking mellows the kraut's flavor and its fermented tang is set off by the sweetness of the fruit.

SERVES 4
Active time: 20 MINUTES
Start to finish: 2½ TO 3½ HOURS

Four 4- to 6-ounce pork cheeks
Kosher salt
1 tablespoon vegetable oil
2 tablespoons unsalted butter
1 large onion, thinly sliced
One 32-ounce bag of sauerkraut, rinsed and drained
2 firm not-too-ripe pears, cored and thinly sliced
1 cup dry white wine
1 cup low-sodium chicken stock

1. Season the pork cheeks all over with ½ teaspoon of salt and let them come to room temperature.

2. Heat the oil in a medium heavy pot over medium-high heat until it shimmers, then sear the pork on both sides until it's richly browned, 4 to 6 minutes total. Transfer the pork to a plate. Stir in the butter and onion and cook, stirring occasionally, until the onion turns golden, about 12 minutes.

3. Stir in the sauerkraut, pears, wine, and stock. Nestle the pork in the mixture, adding any juices from the plate. Let the liquid come to a simmer, cover the pot, and reduce the heat to low to cook at a very gentle simmer until the cheeks are very tender, 2 to 3 hours, depending on whether you like them tender or fall-apart tender.

4. Remove the pot from the heat and let it all hang out for 15 minutes or so. Season with salt to taste.

SAUSAGES WITH BITTER GREENS

AND RED WINE

Slow-cooked pork shoulder, of course, isn't the only gateway meat to good stuff like greens and grains. Sausage offers some of the satisfying richness of shoulder and it's ready quick. And while I'm all for grilling sausages, I'll take mine this way any day, especially in winter. It's a simplified braise, no searing necessary, and a great way to treat sausages while introducing some greens to help round out the meal. They come out plump and porky, just like they're meant to. All you need is a hunk of bread or simply cooked grains to turn this rustic dish into a meal.

SERVES 4 TO 6
Active time: 20 MINUTES
Start to finish: 35 MINUTES

2 tablespoons extra-virgin olive oil

1 medium yellow onion, thinly sliced

3 garlic cloves, smashed and peeled

1 small head of escarole, bruised outer leaves removed

1 small head of radicchio

Kosher salt

1½ pounds Italian-style sausage links

1½ cups dry red wine

1. Heat the oil in a large heavy pot over medium-high heat until it shimmers. Stir in the onion and garlic and cook, stirring occasionally, until the onion turns golden brown, about 8 minutes.

2. Cut the escarole and radicchio each into 8 wedges and add to the pot with ½ teaspoon of salt. Cook, stirring, until the greens have wilted slightly, about 2 minutes. Add the wine and let come to a simmer. Add the sausages and turn the heat to medium-low. Cover and cook at a gentle simmer until the sausage is just cooked through, meaning the pink is gone but the meat is still juicy, 10 to 15 minutes. Season with more salt to taste.

PORK CHOPS

When I'm not slow-cooking pork, I'm grilling or pan-searing it. And when I do, I choose chops almost every time. They cook quickly and pack way more flavor than tenderloin and cutlets. I love all chops, not just the rib chops I call for in the following three recipes, so feel free to substitute less expensive blade chops, which feature both tender and awesomely chewy meat. When you do use rib chops, cook them medium to medium rare. I love it when the interior is rosy.

Each recipe showcases a slightly different way to treat the chops: (1) You can hit them with a last-minute glaze, so they end up sticky and a little sweet; (2) you can rub them with spices, then whip up a sauce whose flavor pairs well with the blend you choose; or (3) you can cook them simply, generously sprinkled with salt, and pair them with a flavorful vegetable dish to be spooned on top like a relish. To take any of these options to the next level, look to a brine (page 199) so the meat ends up especially flavorful and moist.

APPLE CIDER PORK CHOPS

SERVES 4 TO 6
Active time: 25 MINUTES
Start to finish: 4 TO 13 HOURS (IF BRINING)

1 cup apple cider

⅓ cup light brown sugar

2 tablespoons apple cider vinegar

1 teaspoon finely chopped fresh sage or thyme leaves

Kosher salt

Four 6- to 8-ounce 1-inch-thick pork chops (brined, if you like; see page 199), room temperature

1 tablespoon vegetable oil

1. Bring the cider, sugar, vinegar, herbs, and a few pinches of salt to a boil in a small saucepan and boil until slightly syrupy, 6 to 8 minutes. Reserve the glaze.

2. Preheat the oven to 350°F. Line a baking sheet with parchment paper. If the pork isn't already brined, generously season the chops all over with salt.

3. Heat the oil in a large heavy skillet over medium heat until it smokes lightly. Sear the pork chops, in batches if necessary, until golden brown on both sides, about 3 minutes per side. Transfer the pork to the lined baking sheet and brush with some of the sauce. Roast the chops until they're cooked through but still slightly pink in the center, 5 to 8 minutes.

4. Transfer to a serving platter, let rest for 5 minutes or so, and then drizzle on more of the sauce.

SPICED GRILLED PORK CHOPS

WITH CILANTRO YOGURT

An Indian-inspired spice rub—cumin, coriander, turmeric, and cardamom—gives these chops a heady flavor. Easy cilantro-yogurt sauce is a cool, herbaceous complement to the chops' complexity.

SERVES 4 TO 6
Active time: **25 MINUTES**
Start to finish: **4 TO 13 HOURS (IF BRINING)**

Grapeseed or vegetable oil, for the grill

1 cup whole-milk yogurt

1 cup packed very coarsely chopped fresh cilantro

1 to 2 tablespoons fresh lime juice

Kosher salt

1 teaspoon ground coriander

1 teaspoon ground cumin

½ teaspoon ground turmeric

¼ teaspoon ground cardamom

Freshly ground black pepper

Four 6- to 8-ounce 1-inch-thick pork chops (brined, if you like; see page 199), room temperature

1. Preheat a gas or charcoal grill so there's an area of medium heat and low heat. Pour a little oil on a rag, grab the rag with tongs, and rub the oil onto the grill grates to prevent sticking.

2. Pulse the yogurt, cilantro, 1 tablespoon of the lime juice, and ½ teaspoon of salt in a food processor until smooth. Season to taste with more lime juice.

3. In a small bowl, stir together the coriander, cumin, turmeric, cardamom, 2 teaspoons of salt (if the pork isn't already brined), and ½ teaspoon pepper. Rub the spice mixture all over the pork chops.

4. Grill the chops over medium heat, flipping occasionally and moving them to the low-heat area if they threaten to get too dark, until cooked through but still slightly pink in the center, 10 to 15 minutes. Transfer the pork to a serving platter and let rest for 5 minutes, then serve with the cilantro yogurt.

PORK CHOPS WITH TOMATO CORN RELISH

These pork chops match perfectly with a dead-simple relish of corn that's sautéed in the porky fat left in the skillet. Mixed with summer tomatoes and fresh herbs, the corn makes a fresh, sweet-sour accompaniment to the rich chops.

SERVES 4 TO 6
Active time: 20 MINUTES
Start to finish: 30 MINUTES TO 12 HOURS (IF BRINING)

Four 6- to 8-ounce 1-inch-thick pork chops (brined, if you like; see page 199), room temperature

Kosher salt

1 tablespoon vegetable oil

4 ears corn, shucked, kernels removed (see page 63)

1 pint cherry tomatoes, halved, or 2 medium tomatoes, cored and chopped

½ cup torn fresh basil leaves

1 tablespoon coarsely chopped fresh dill

2 tablespoons apple cider vinegar

1. Preheat the oven to 350°F. Line a baking sheet with parchment paper.

2. If they're not already brined, generously season the pork chops all over with salt. Heat the oil in a large heavy skillet over medium heat until it smokes lightly. Sear the pork chops, in batches if necessary, until golden brown on both sides, about 3 minutes per side. Transfer the pork to the lined baking sheet. Roast the chops until they're cooked through but still slightly pink in the center, 8 to 10 minutes.

3. While the pork roasts, add the corn to the hot skillet over medium heat and cook until cooked and crisp-tender, stirring occasionally and scraping up any browned bits, about 3 minutes. Add the tomatoes and cook until just warmed through, about 1 minute. Transfer the corn to a bowl and stir in the basil, dill, vinegar, and ½ teaspoon of salt.

4. Transfer the pork chops to a serving platter and let rest for 5 minutes or so. Serve with the tomato-corn relish.

JUST A LITTLE BEEF—BUT MAKE IT GOOD

AS THE SUN SET on Election Day 2008, then-senator Barack Obama, Michelle, and their family gathered at the couple's home in Chicago. He had given the stump speeches, done the meet-and-greets, and headlined the fund-raisers. He played a good-luck game of basketball. Now there was nothing left to do but have dinner.

And that was my job. I had planned a dinner for a celebratory occasion—a few monster rib eyes, a salad of shaved fennel and citrus, wild rice, and pie for dessert.

I jumped in my car, drove toward downtown to a supermarket with a solid meat selection, and asked the butcher to grab half a rib section's-worth of dry-aged beef. I watched as he hoisted a rack on his shoulder and hauled it to the cutting board. His back to me, he started trimming it and sliced it in half, then abruptly stopped working. When he quietly but urgently summoned the other guys behind the counter, I got worried that something was wrong. "Hey, you all right?" I called to him. He snapped to, suddenly remembering I was there, and turned to me holding a slab of meat dappled with so much white fat I could've been looking at top-grade, $200-a-pound Kobe beef. Any rib eye worth its price has some nice marbling, but this was insane—the steak equivalent of a winning lottery ticket. "I've never seen anything like this," he told me. "Whoever you're cooking for is one lucky guy."

I probably smiled a bit too big as he wrapped up my order. A chill down my spine, I headed back toward the home of the man who just a few hours later, would no longer be called "Senator" but "President-elect." Halfway there, I hit the brakes, turned around, and went back to the butcher to buy the other half of that rib section. You only get that lucky once. Or at least, once every four years.

GRILLED RIB EYE

WITH FOUR SAUCES

You don't have to make beef election-night-only food in order to curb your consumption. But if you treat it as special-occasion food, make sure that the beef is special, too. My take is a riff on the classic beer commercial line: I don't usually eat steak, but when I do, I prefer rib eye. In other words, eat less beef; but when you do, choose the beefiest, most luscious stuff you can find. You might be into the slightly less fatty strip; the appealingly chewy, beefy skirt; or tender flat-iron and hanger. Or, of course, there's nothing better than an awesome burger. No matter what you like best, cooking steak requires nothing but salt, pepper, and a hot grill. Your goal is simple: to give it a nice brown crust and pull it just *before* it's cooked the way you like it—as it rests, the juices redistribute and the temperature inside creeps up.

You'll notice that I say that two 1-pound steaks serve 4 to 6 people. If your brow just furrowed, I hear you: I can take down a whole rib eye by myself, too. But in the interest of treating beef as an indulgence rather than a staple, I like to serve less per person and make up the difference with plenty of whole grains and vegetables. And even though I *can* eat twice that amount of steak, I've got to say I feel so much better when I don't.

IS IT DONE?

Knowing when a steak is done is easy—if you've cooked it hundreds of times. With experience comes an almost supernatural power to prod a steak with your finger, or even just to glance at it, and tell that it's cooked to medium rare. If you haven't, there's a cool trick that helps. Holding one palm up, touch your thumb to your index finger, and with the other hand, poke the fleshy area under your thumb. That slight give and spring? That's what a medium-rare steak feels like. Now touch your thumb to your middle finger and do the same—that's what medium feels like. Your ring finger and that's medium-well; your pinky and that's well-done.

Because everyone's definition of a hot grill or pan is different, start occasionally poking the center of each steak a few minutes before the recipe suggests it'll be ready. After several goes, you'll learn to associate the feeling with the color you see when you ultimately slice it.

BUYING BEEF

It's true that meat from cows who eat grass all their lives is better for the planet (and for the animals) than meat from those who spend the last few months of their lives fattening up on grain. It's also true that a diet of all grass tends to make for meat that's leaner and stronger in flavor than the stuff most of us are used to. For some people, that's a tough sell, especially because the price is often higher to boot. The good news is that farmers are getting better at the task, producing meat with milder flavor and good marbling. So if you haven't already, try some—and because it's lean, take extra care to keep it rare to medium rare. If you're dead set on grain-finished steak, you can still do your part by eating less of it.

SERVES 2 TO 3
Active time: 15 MINUTES
Start to finish: 25 MINUTES

One 1-pound bone-in rib eye steak, about 1½ inch thick

Kosher salt and freshly ground black pepper

Grapeseed or vegetable oil

1. Let the steak come to room temperature. Pat it very dry and generously season all over with salt and pepper. The thicker the cut, the heavier I go on the salt and pepper to make up for the higher ratio of unseasoned interior to seasoned exterior.

2A. ON THE GRILL: Preheat a gas or charcoal grill to high heat. Pour a little oil on a rag, grab the rag with tongs, and rub the oil onto the grill grates to prevent sticking.

Grill the steak on one side until golden brown and charred in spots, rotating them 90 degrees to keep the color even, 4 to 6 minutes. Stand by with tongs in hand, moving the steaks whenever there's a flare-up; if your steak is fatty, there will be some. Flip the steaks and grill, rotating, until they're cooked the way you like (see "Is It Done?" on page 217), 4 to 6 minutes more for medium rare to medium.

2B. AT THE STOVE: Add a slick of oil to a large heavy ovenproof skillet wide enough to hold both steaks with room to spare, and use a paper towel to rub the oil to coat the surface. Set the skillet over medium-high heat until the oil begins to smoke. Add the steak and cook, rotating it once to keep the color even, until the bottom is deep golden brown, about 3 minutes. Flip the steak and cook for about 4 minutes for medium rare and 5 to 6 minutes for medium.

3. Let the steak rest for 5 to 10 minutes, then carve off the bone, but don't discard it. Cut the steak against the grain into thick slices. Serve the slices on a platter with the meaty bone for those who love gnawing it.

BETTER STEAK SAUCES

When I want to simplify my dinner duty, I skip the marinades, brines, and dry rubs and employ the underrated season-with-salt-then-cook technique of preparing steak. Instead of focusing on adding flavor to the meat itself, I use my energy to make sure it's generously seasoned and well cooked. For brightness, heat, and fun, I look to an array of sauces to take the simply cooked meat in different exciting directions.

CHIMICHURRI

This bright, herb-jammed sauce—like a souped-up vinaigrette—goes well with anything, but the puckery acidity and fresh flavor make an especially good partner to fat-riddled rib eye.

MAKES ABOUT 1½ CUPS
Active time: **10 MINUTES**
Start to finish: **10 MINUTES**

2 garlic cloves, finely chopped
Kosher salt
1 small shallot, finely chopped
⅓ cup red wine vinegar
¼ cup roughly chopped fresh cilantro
¼ cup roughly chopped fresh parsley
Several big pinches of finely chopped fresh oregano leaves
¼ to 1 teaspoon finely chopped fresh red chile
½ cup extra-virgin olive oil

Set the garlic on a cutting board, add a pinch of salt, and use the flat side of a chef's knife to mash it to a paste. Scrape it into a bowl and stir in the shallot, vinegar, and 1 teaspoon of salt. Let it sit for 5 minutes or so or up to an hour. Right before you serve the sauce, stir in the herbs, chile, and oil. Season to taste with salt and serve it with the steak.

HORSERADISH AND PARSLEY

CHIMICHURRI
CHERRY STEAK SAUCE
GREEN TOMATO SALSA VERDE

HORSERADISH
AND PARSLEY

The sting of horseradish makes this simple condiment of chopped parsley, garlic, and lemon zest (what the French would call *persillade*) even more welcome with steak.

MAKES A SCANT ¾ CUP
Active time: 10 MINUTES
Start to finish: 10 MINUTES

½ cup finely chopped fresh parsley
¼ cup finely grated fresh or drained prepared horseradish
1 tablespoon finely grated lemon zest
1 garlic clove, finely chopped
Kosher salt

Stir together the parsley, horseradish, lemon zest, garlic, and ½ teaspoon of salt until combined. Scatter the mixture over the steak slices right before serving.

GREEN TOMATO
SALSA VERDE

Battering and frying isn't the only way to prepare green tomatoes. I treat these summer castoffs as if they were tomatillos, making a lively salsa out of the crisp, tart fruit.

MAKES ABOUT 1½ CUPS
Active time: 5 MINUTES
Start to finish: 5 MINUTES

1 pound unripe green tomatoes, cored and coarsely chopped
½ cup packed very coarsely chopped fresh cilantro or parsley
1 serrano or jalapeño chile, finely chopped (for less heat, remove the veins and seeds)
2 tablespoons fresh lime juice
Kosher salt

Combine the tomatoes, cilantro, chile, lime juice, and 1 teaspoon of salt in a food processor. Pulse until fairly finely chopped and well combined. Season with more salt to taste and serve with the steak.

CHERRY STEAK SAUCE

I'm so down with the kind of sweet sauce you tend to find at old-school steak houses with sawdust on the floor, tuxedos on the waiters, and beef fat in the air. But when I make my own, I look to the sultry sweetness of cherries and the complexity of red wine to make a version that's less sugary and more flavorful.

MAKES ABOUT 2 CUPS
Active time: 15 MINUTES
Start to finish: 25 MINUTES

1 tablespoon extra-virgin olive oil

1 medium yellow onion, chopped

1 medium red bell pepper, seeded, deveined, and chopped

2 garlic cloves, smashed

Kosher salt

1 tablespoon tomato paste

1 teaspoon ground cumin

1½ cups fresh or thawed frozen pitted sweet cherries

¼ cup dry red wine

2 tablespoons apple cider vinegar

1 tablespoon brown sugar

1. Heat the oil in a large heavy skillet over medium-high heat until it shimmers. Stir in the onion, pepper, garlic, and ½ teaspoon salt and cook, stirring occasionally, until the peppers are tender, 10 to 12 minutes. Stir in the tomato paste and cumin and cook, stirring constantly, until the tomato paste turns a few shades darker, about 1 minute. Stir in the cherries and ½ teaspoon salt and cook, stirring, until softened, about 4 minutes. Stir in the wine, vinegar, and sugar. Transfer the mixture to a blender, and blend until smooth.

2. Return the sauce to the skillet, bring to a simmer over medium heat, and cook until it's a little looser than ketchup, 2 to 4 minutes. Season with more salt and sugar to taste and serve with the steak.

EAT
MORE
GRAINS
AND BEANS

I DON'T NEED another reason to eat more farro. Because when you sweat onions in butter, stir in the grain, and slowly simmer it with stock, as if you were making risotto, farro takes on a bold, nutty flavor and hearty chew that gives Arborio rice a run for its money. I don't need another reason to eat more lentils, because after they've been cooked until tender and tossed with sweet summer tomatoes, grated zucchini, herbs, and sweet-tart balsamic, a spoonful tells me all I need to know. I don't need another reason to make a pot of black beans spiked with lime and smoky chipotle chiles, because the earthy, savory, creamy result is crazy good. To me, eating this stuff is about pleasure, not penance. In every bite, there is love and happiness.

So I don't ever feel like I *need* another reason to eat more whole grains and beans, but man, are there some great ones. The details are surprising, fascinating, and even a little bizarre. If you're not interested, skip them and flip the page to find almost three dozen recipes for simple, delicious food anchored by a handful of these unsung ingredients, which taste as good as they are for you and for the planet. But if you're intrigued, then before you dig in, let's dig in.

First up, whole grains and members of the legume family, including beans, lentils, and chickpeas, are really good for you. I know: You've heard that before. But it deserves repeating. Like fruits and vegetables, they're nutrient dense, providing the kind of calories you can consume with the knowledge you're eating well. And they provide a big dose of fiber. (For more on why that matters, see page 30.)

Next, whole grains and beans represent one of the coolest convergences between our bodies' health and the planet's. They're great for you, and when you eat more of them, farmers plant more of them. And you help unleash a powerful weapon in improving the soil.

Take legumes, aka beans, as an example. Synthetic fertilizers are one of the backbones of the current agricultural system and have a major impact on greenhouse gas emissions, but beans can help mitigate that problem. These fertilizers employ nitrogen, which is vital for plant growth. Then, in the process of planting and harvesting, the gas is released in the form of nitrous oxide, which has a heat-trapping effect, oh, several hundred times greater than carbon dioxide's. And that's before we get to the problem of all that fertilizer ending up in our rivers and oceans, wreaking havoc and creating "dead zones."

But legumes offer a better way to feed the soil. They play an important role in what's called crop rotation. Instead of growing the same crop in the same place year after year, which is how most industrial agriculture works, farmers plant different crops in the same fields through the seasons. Each crop serves a different purpose, often to replenish something in the soil that a previous crop took up. For legumes, that something is nitrogen. Basically, they've got a deal with bacteria in the soil, and through a process more complicated than you or I need to worry about, they enrich soil with nitrogen rather than deplete it. More nitrogen in the soil means less need for those fertilizers.

And it's not just legumes. Other crops benefit soil in different ways. Grains like wheat and barley, for instance, help curb weeds and build structure and balance in soil. Healthy soil also traps carbon from the air, pulling bad stuff from the air into the ground.

The crop rotation method of farming is by far the better way, the healthier and more sustainable way. But it's not, frankly, the easier way. So farmers need your help. I know I say over and over that one of the best ways to do that is to eat more vegetables in general, and I stand by that. But we can do even more good if we eat more broadly than the sexy plants like tomatoes and asparagus. By eating more grains and legumes—both in amount and in variety—you help build a market for these ingredients, and you help create a virtuous cycle of better agriculture. (For more on this idea, I highly recommend a tremendous book called *The Third Plate* by Dan Barber, founder and chef of the famous restaurant Blue Hill at Stone Barns just outside New York City.)

That's why in this chapter, I'll introduce you to some of my favorite ways to cook the good-for-us gang. I take you through four seasonal riffs on each one—a fun way to treat ingredients that keep in your pantry all year round—and often pack in the vegetables, from raw to roasted, to add flavor and texture. You'll find a ton of ideas here, and they're almost all interchangeable. For instance, the roasted beets, arugula, and Parm that I add to whole-wheat couscous or the pomegranate seeds, pistachios, and orange zest I toss with bulgur are going to rock with lentils, quinoa, and brown rice, too. So in addition to the recipes themselves, I share a dead-simple way to cook each grain or legume and how to store it. That way, it's easy to have good stuff ready to go in your fridge. Then you can mix and match grains, vegetables, flavors, and textures, and do right by yourself and everyone else.

FOUR WAYS WITH FRIED RICE

One of the first dishes I ever cooked was fried rice—sort of. When I was a kid, we almost always had leftover rice hanging around in the fridge. I'd often come home hungry from playing whatever sport I was hooked on at the time, get some butter and a heap of rice in the microwave, and season it with soy sauce and Parmesan for an umami-bomb of a snack. As I got older, I upped my game, paying homage to fried rice's originators by using ginger, garlic, and scallions, and then packing in whatever vegetables I had in the fridge. Nowadays, I use the dish's basic magic—the reviving of grains with heat and fat—to make an array of one-plate meals that often have little else in common with the kind of dish you'd gobble alongside wonton soup and shrimp in black bean sauce. I use brown rice, not just because it's better for me but because I love the nutty flavor and chew. Slip a fried egg on top for the healthy protein and richness it brings.

SIMPLE BROWN RICE

Rice is notoriously tricky to get right on the stovetop. Different crops spend different amounts of time on the shelf to be cooked using different definitions of "low heat." Mushiness often ensues. Well, not with these two techniques.

MAKES THREE TIMES AS MUCH COOKED BROWN RICE AS DRIED

ON THE STOVETOP: Skip all the fuss of finding the exact ratio of rice to water by cooking it like pasta. Bring a large pot of water to a boil. Meanwhile, give the grains a quick rinse and drain. When the water reaches a boil, stir in the rice and cook, stirring occasionally, until the grains are tender with a slight chew, usually 25 to 30 minutes. Drain it in a strainer with small holes so you don't lose any rice, then return it to the empty pot. Cover the rice with a clean kitchen towel, then the lid, and let sit for 5 minutes.

IN A RICE COOKER: Even an inexpensive rice cooker makes exceptional brown rice. Give the grains a quick rinse, drain well, and put them in the rice cooker. Add water according to the ratio suggested on the bag (I usually add just a bit less, so my rice has a little more chew). Close the lid, and press the button. When it's finished cooking, gently fluff the rice to help keep it from cooking further and getting mushy.

Use the rice right away or let it cool. It's great hot or at room temperature. Once cooled, it keeps in an airtight container in the fridge for up to 5 days.

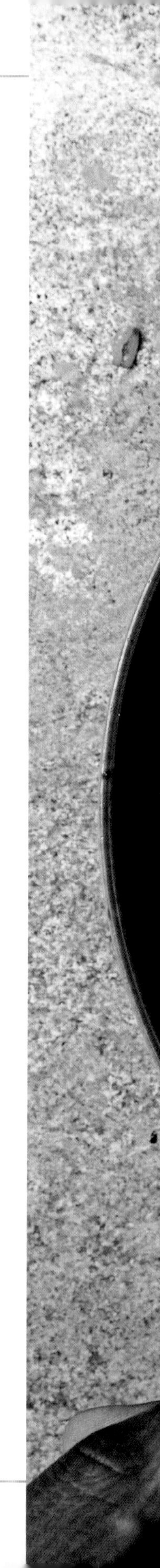

PUT AN EGG ON IT

A fried egg or two takes brown rice—or really any grain, bean, or vegetable dish—from a side to a meal, and there's no quicker, easier way. Once the egg hits hot fat, you're a minute or so away from sunny-side-up perfection, fluffy whites and a molten yolk that sauces grilled asparagus or stewed lentils or wild rice, adding its luxurious richness—not to mention lean protein with relatively low environmental impact. Here's how I make mine:

Cook 1 or 2 eggs at a time. Any more than that gets tricky. Use a nonstick skillet unless you have a trusty well-seasoned pan.

Unless you're a real pro, crack them into a bowl first and fish out any bits of shell. Heat a splash of olive oil in a small skillet over medium-high heat until it shimmers. Slide the egg into the skillet and reduce the heat to medium (or if you're like my wife, Alex, keep cooking on medium high so the edges get brown and crispy). Season with salt and cook until the top of the whites set and the yolks are nice and runny, 2 to 3 minutes.

SPRING

FRIED BROWN RICE WITH KOHLRABI, AVOCADO, AND SPROUTS

SERVES 4 TO 6
Active time: 20 MINUTES
Start to finish: 20 MINUTES

¼ cup extra-virgin olive oil
3 cups peeled, diced (about ½-inch) kohlrabi, turnip, or radish
Kosher salt
3 cups cooked and cooled brown rice (page 230)
1 tablespoon soy sauce
2 ripe avocados, sliced
Handful of alfalfa or bean sprouts
1 fried egg per person (see page 231)

1. Heat the oil in a large wok or nonstick skillet over medium-high heat until it shimmers. Stir in the kohlrabi and ½ teaspoon salt and cook, stirring frequently, until crisp-tender, about 6 minutes. Add the rice and cook, breaking up clumps and stirring only occasionally, until the rice is heated through and crispy in spots, about 10 minutes.

2. Sprinkle the soy sauce evenly over the rice, stir well, and season with salt to taste. Divide the rice among bowls with the avocado, sprouts, and fried eggs on top.

SUMMER

SMOKY FRIED BROWN RICE WITH OKRA, SAUSAGE, AND TOMATO

SERVES 4 TO 6
Active time: 20 MINUTES
Start to finish: 20 MINUTES

1 pint okra or trimmed green beans or snap peas
¼ cup vegetable oil
¾ pound smoked sausage, such as andouille or kielbasa, cut into ½-inch slices
Kosher salt
3 cups cooked and cooled brown rice (page 230)
1 teaspoon smoked paprika
1 large tomato, cored and chopped
1 fried egg per person (see page 231)

1. Remove the stems from the okra, cutting along the line at the fat part of the seed pod. Trimming okra this way avoids exposing the seeds and spares everyone from the vegetable's dreaded slime.

2. Heat the oil in a large wok or nonstick skillet over medium-high heat until it shimmers. Add the sausage and brown it for about 1 minute per side. Transfer to a plate, leaving the fat behind. Stir the okra and ½ to 1 teaspoon of salt into the skillet and cook, stirring frequently, until bright green and tender, 3 to 5 minutes. Transfer the okra to the plate with the sausage.

3. Add the rice to the skillet and cook, breaking up clumps and stirring only occasionally, until the rice is heated through and crispy in spots, about 10 minutes. Sprinkle on the paprika and cook until fragrant. Stir in the tomato, sausage, and okra and season with salt to taste. Divide the rice mixture among bowls and top each with a fried egg.

FALL

FRIED BROWN RICE WITH MUSHROOMS AND EDAMAME

SERVES 4 TO 6
Active time: 20 MINUTES
Start to finish: 20 MINUTES

⅓ cup peanut oil
¼ pound shiitake mushrooms, stemmed and sliced
1 cup fresh or thawed frozen shelled edamame
Kosher salt
1 tablespoon peeled and finely chopped fresh ginger
2 garlic cloves, finely chopped
3 cups cooked and cooled brown rice (page 230)
1 tablespoon soy sauce
2 scallions, thinly sliced
1 fried egg per person (see page 231)

1. Heat the oil in a large wok or nonstick skillet over medium-high heat until it shimmers. Stir in the mushrooms and cook, stirring frequently, until tender and golden brown, about 4 minutes. Stir in the edamame and ½ to 1 teaspoon of salt and cook, stirring frequently, until hot, about 2 minutes. Stir in the ginger and garlic and cook, stirring, until the garlic turns golden, about 2 minutes.

2. Add the rice and cook, breaking up clumps and stirring only occasionally until the rice is heated through and crispy in spots, about 10 minutes. Sprinkle on the soy sauce, stir well, and season with more salt to taste. Divide the rice among bowls and top with the scallions and fried eggs.

WINTER

FRIED BROWN RICE WITH BUTTERNUT SQUASH AND KALE

SERVES 4 TO 6
Active time: 20 MINUTES
Start to finish: 45 MINUTES

1 medium (about 2 pounds) butternut squash, peeled, seeded, and cut into ½-inch cubes
½ cup extra-virgin olive oil
Kosher salt
1 medium bunch kale, stem bottoms trimmed, cut into bite-sized pieces
3 cups cooked and cooled brown rice (page 230)
2 tablespoons peeled and finely chopped ginger
1 tablespoon soy sauce
¼ cup toasted pumpkin seeds
1 fried egg per person (see page 231)

1. Preheat the oven to 425°F. On a baking sheet, toss the squash with 2 tablespoons of the oil and ½ to ¾ teaspoon of salt. Spread it out into one layer and roast until tender and browned, about 25 minutes. Set aside.

2. Heat the remaining 6 tablespoons oil in a large wok or nonstick skillet over medium-high heat until it shimmers. Stir in the kale and ½ to 1 teaspoon of salt and cook, stirring frequently, until tender, 6 to 8 minutes adding a few splashes of water if needed. Add the rice and ginger and cook, breaking up clumps and stirring only occasionally until the rice is heated through and crispy in spots, about 10 minutes. Fold in as much of the squash as you like. Sprinkle on the soy sauce, stir well, and season with more salt to taste. Divide the rice among bowls and top with the pumpkin seeds and fried eggs.

FOUR WAYS WITH QUINOA

Do believe the hype. Cultivated by the Incas millennia ago, this seed has journeyed from the mountains of Peru to dusty shelves at Berkeley health food stores to a supermarket near you. All the fanfare is deserved—it tastes great and it's full of good stuff. In fact, it's one of the only plant-based complete proteins, meaning it includes all the amino acids you'd get (and that your body needs) from meat and eggs. It's quick and easy to make, too. Instead of messing with precise ratios of water to quinoa, I cook it like pasta, draining it when it's tender but still has the soft pop that makes it such a pleasure to eat. Then I toss it with whatever good stuff I have on hand—like snap peas and fava beans in the spring, zucchini and eggplant in the summer, squash and pecans in the fall, and parsnips and Meyer lemon (peel, slightly sweet flesh, and all) in the winter.

SIMPLE QUINOA

You can cook quinoa the same way you cook rice (with a ratio of 1 part quinoa to 1½ to 2 parts water or stock), but I like to cook it like pasta. Serve it hot and buttered, cold and tossed with vegetables, or any way in between.

MAKES THREE TIMES AS MUCH COOKED QUINOA AS DRIED

1. Bring a large pot of water to a boil. Meanwhile, put the quinoa in a fine-mesh strainer and rinse really well under cold water.

2. When the water reaches a boil, add salt so the water tastes slightly salty, stir in the quinoa, and cook, stirring occasionally, until it's tender with a slight pop to the grains, 10 to 15 minutes. Drain in a fine-mesh strainer. Transfer the quinoa to a baking sheet or very large plate and spread it out a bit to cool slightly. This helps keep it from cooking further and getting mushy.

3. Use the quinoa right away or let cool. It's great hot or cold. Once cooled, it keeps in an airtight container in the fridge for up to 5 days.

SPRING

QUINOA SALAD WITH SNAP PEAS

SERVES 4 TO 6
Active time: 20 MINUTES
Start to finish: 20 MINUTES

3 tablespoons extra-virgin olive oil

1 small shallot, thinly sliced

1 cup snap peas, strings removed (see below), sliced diagonally (blanched, peeled favas or edamame also work well)

Kosher salt

3 cups cooked quinoa (page 236)

Small handful of torn fresh basil leaves

2 to 3 tablespoons white balsamic or white wine vinegar

1. Heat the oil in a large heavy skillet over medium heat until it shimmers. Stir in the shallot and cook, stirring occasionally, until translucent, about 4 minutes. Stir in the peas and a few pinches of salt. Cook, stirring occasionally, until the peas are bright green and crisp-tender, 3 minutes. Remove the skillet from the heat.

2. Stir in the quinoa. Let everything cool to warm or room temperature, then fold in the basil, vinegar, and salt to taste.

SNAP PEA STRINGS: Snap peas in spring taste like candy from the earth, naturally sweet and irresistibly crisp. All you need to do before you eat them is remove the strings. One by one, hold the snap peas stem-side up so they curve toward you. Use a small knife to cut just under the tip of the stem, then pull the tip toward you to remove the string that runs the length of the snap pea. Repeat on the other end to remove the strings along the spine.

SUMMER

QUINOA SALAD WITH RATATOUILLE VEGETABLES

SERVES 4 TO 6
Active time: 20 MINUTES
Start to finish: 20 MINUTES

¼ cup extra-virgin olive oil

1 medium eggplant, cut into ¾-inch pieces

Kosher salt

3 cups cooked quinoa (page 236)

1 red bell pepper, stemmed, seeded, and cut into ½-inch pieces

1 medium zucchini, cut into ¾-inch pieces

1 cup chopped tomatoes or halved cherry tomatoes

Handful of coarsely chopped fresh parsley

2 to 3 tablespoons red wine vinegar

1. Heat 2 tablespoons of the oil in a large heavy skillet over medium heat until it just begins to smoke. Add the eggplant in one layer and ½ teaspoon of salt. Cook, stirring occasionally, until tender, 8 to 10 minutes. In a large serving bowl, combine the eggplant and the quinoa.

2. Raise the heat to medium high, pour the remaining 2 tablespoons oil into the skillet, and cook the bell pepper and zucchini with a generous pinch of salt until crisp-tender, about 6 minutes. Toss them with the quinoa and eggplant and let everything cool to warm or room temperature. Fold in the tomatoes, parsley, vinegar, and salt to taste, and serve.

FALL

QUINOA SALAD WITH SQUASH AND TOASTED PECANS

SERVES 4 TO 6
Active time: 20 MINUTES
Start to finish: 20 MINUTES

1 medium red onion, thinly sliced into half-moons

Kosher salt

½ cup distilled white vinegar, or more if necessary

5 tablespoons extra-virgin olive oil

2 cups diced (about ¾-inch) peeled kabocha or butternut squash

3 cups cooked red quinoa (page 236; red quinoa make take a few minutes longer to cook than white)

½ cup pecans, toasted, coarsely chopped

Handful of roughly chopped fresh parsley

1. Combine the onion, 1 teaspoon of salt, and enough vinegar to just cover the onion in a bowl, and mix until the salt dissolves. Let the onion pickle while you finish the dish.

2. Heat 3 tablespoons of the oil in a large heavy skillet over medium heat until it shimmers. Stir in the squash and ½ teaspoon of salt and cook, stirring occasionally, until tender, 8 to 10 minutes.

3. In a large serving bowl, toss the squash with the quinoa. Drain the onion and add it to the bowl. Let everything cool to warm or room temperature, then fold in the pecans, parsley, remaining 2 tablespoons oil, and salt to taste.

WINTER

QUINOA SALAD WITH PARSNIPS AND MEYER LEMON

SERVES 4 TO 6
Active time: 20 MINUTES
Start to finish: 20 MINUTES

3 tablespoons extra-virgin olive oil

2 large parsnips, peeled and cut into ½-inch pieces

Kosher salt

3 cups cooked quinoa (page 236)

1 Meyer lemon (see below), washed well

3 celery stalks, thinly sliced, plus some leaves

½ teaspoon dried red pepper flakes

1. Heat the oil in a large heavy skillet over medium heat until it shimmers. Stir in the parsnips and ¼ to ½ teaspoon of salt and cook, stirring occasionally, until tender, 8 to 10 minutes. In a large serving bowl, toss the parsnips with the quinoa.

2. Cut the lemon into thin slices, flick out the seeds, and finely chop it, rind and all. Fold the lemon into the quinoa along with the sliced celery and the pepper flakes. Let everything cool to warm or room temperature, then season with more salt to taste. Scatter on the celery leaves.

MEYER LEMONS: The Meyer lemon's acidity is mellower and its flavor more complex than that of a regular lemon. Look for it from winter to early spring in fancy supermarkets, or farmer's markets if you're in California.

FOUR WAYS WITH FARRO

I started swapping farro (also known as emmer wheat) for the traditional Arborio rice in my risotto to bump up the dish's health status, but I kept on doing it because of how good it gets when you cook it slowly with stock. Don't tell my Italian friends, but now I downright prefer to use these nutty, chewy grains instead of rice. When you cook them this way, they do release a little starch (though not as much as rice does) to give the dish a slightly creamy texture.

Here I share four of my favorite ways to vary things, one for each season. In springtime, I add asparagus and sweet peas. When summer comes, I stir in spinach pesto for a vivid green color and top-notch cherry tomatoes to deliver a sweet-tart burst in every bite. For fall, I let meaty mushrooms brown in the oven, then enrich the dish with a dollop of crème fraîche, sour cream's richer cousin. During winter, I look to sweet shellfish, like scallops and shrimp, to turn this side dish into centerpiece. Most farro is sold pearled or semi-pearled—that is, with all or some of the bran removed—both of which cook more quickly but have fewer nutrients than whole-grain farro. When I have the time, I go for the latter, though semi-pearled is great, too.

SIMPLE FARRO

Even if you don't prepare the farro risotto-style, there are countless ways to use simply cooked farro. It can serve as the base for virtually any of the grain preparations in this chapter, or as a side, simply seasoned with olive oil and salt, maybe with a splash of vinegar and a handful of chopped herbs. Here's how to make farro at its most basic. This method simplifies the task by forgoing the precise ratios of grain to water without sacrificing any of the great chewy texture or nutty flavor.

MAKES TWICE AS MUCH COOKED FARRO AS DRIED

1. Bring a large pot of water to a boil, add salt so the water tastes slightly salty, and stir in the farro. Reduce the heat to maintain a steady simmer and cook, stirring occasionally, until it's pleasantly chewy, 20 to 30 minutes.

2. Drain. Use it right away or let cool—it's great hot, warm, or cold. Once cooled, it keeps in an airtight container in the fridge for up to 5 days.

BASIC FARRO RISOTTO

SERVES 4 TO 6
Active time: 45 MINUTES
Start to finish: 45 MINUTES

6 to 8 cups low-sodium vegetable or chicken stock
2 tablespoons unsalted butter
1 small onion, finely chopped
2 cups whole-grain or semi-pearled farro
½ cup dry white wine
Kosher salt
Olive oil, to finish
Grated Parmesan, to finish

1. Bring the stock to a simmer in a medium saucepan over medium-high heat, then reduce the heat to keep it at a bare simmer.

2. Melt the butter in a medium heavy pot over medium heat until it froths. Stir in the onion and cook, stirring occasionally, until translucent, about 4 minutes. Stir in the farro and cook, stirring, for 1 minute. Stir in the wine and 1 teaspoon of salt and simmer, stirring, until the wine has almost completely evaporated, about 3 minutes.

3. Stir in about 4 cups of the stock and cook, stirring frequently, until the stock is almost entirely absorbed. Continue adding the stock a cup at a time and stirring frequently until the farro is tender, about 25 minutes total for semi-pearled and about 45 minutes for whole-grain. Season with salt to taste and eat immediately with olive oil and Parmesan to taste, or trick it out with any of the combinations that follow.

SPRING

FARRO RISOTTO WITH ASPARAGUS, PEAS, AND PARMESAN

SERVES 4 TO 6
Active time: 45 MINUTES
Start to finish: 45 MINUTES

1 batch Basic Farro Risotto (page 241), warm
1 bunch of asparagus, tough bottoms trimmed, cut into 1-inch pieces
1 cup shelled fresh or frozen peas
A splash of low-sodium vegetable or chicken stock (optional)
Big handful of finely grated Parmesan cheese
¼ cup extra-virgin olive oil
Kosher salt

When the farro risotto is ready, stir in the asparagus and peas and simmer, still over medium heat, until they're crisp-tender and heated through, about 3 minutes. Add a little more stock or hot water if you'd like the risotto a bit saucier, then remove it from heat and stir in the cheese and oil. Season with salt to taste and serve right away.

SUMMER

FARRO RISOTTO WITH SPINACH PESTO, CHERRY TOMATOES, AND ALMONDS

SERVES 4 TO 6
Active time: 45 MINUTES
Start to finish: 45 MINUTES

1 garlic clove, coarsely chopped
3 cups packed baby spinach
Big handful of finely grated Parmesan cheese
¾ cup almonds, toasted and sliced or coarsely chopped
Kosher salt
⅓ cup extra-virgin olive oil
1 batch Basic Farro Risotto (page 241), warm
1 cup cherry or grape tomatoes, halved
2 tablespoons fresh lemon juice

1. Drop the garlic clove into a food processor with the motor running and process until finely chopped. Add the spinach, Parmesan, ½ cup of the almonds, and ½ teaspoon of salt and pulse to a coarse puree. With the motor running, slowly pour in the oil and process until pretty smooth. The pesto keeps in an airtight container in the fridge for up to 2 days.

2. Off the heat, stir the spinach pesto into the farro risotto. Season with salt to taste, add the tomatoes, the remaining ¼ cup of the almonds, and the lemon juice and serve right away.

FALL

FARRO RISOTTO WITH MUSHROOMS

SERVES 4 TO 6
Active time: 45 MINUTES
Start to finish: 45 MINUTES

1 pound assorted mushrooms, trimmed of tough stems and cut into bite-sized pieces

¼ cup extra-virgin olive oil

Kosher salt

1 batch Basic Farro Risotto (page 241), warm

Big handful of finely grated Parmesan cheese

½ cup crème fraîche

A splash of low-sodium vegetable or chicken stock (optional)

1 tablespoon chopped fresh chives or scallions

1. Before you cook the farro risotto, preheat the oven to 425°F. On a baking sheet, coat the mushrooms in the oil and season with 1 teaspoon of salt. Spread the mushrooms out in a single layer and roast until tender and browned at the edges, 20 to 30 minutes.

2. Make the risotto and stir in the mushrooms and simmer for a minute. Add a little stock or hot water if you'd like the risotto a bit saucier, then remove it from heat and stir in the cheese and crème fraîche. Season with salt to taste and serve right away with chives on top.

WINTER

FARRO RISOTTO WITH SEAFOOD, HERBS, AND LEMON

SERVES 4 TO 6
Active time: 55 MINUTES
Start to finish: 55 MINUTES

1 batch Basic Farro Risotto (page 241), warm

¾ pound medium shrimp, peeled

¾ pound bay scallops or large scallops cut into quarters (see below)

Kosher salt

Big pinch of coarsely chopped fresh tarragon or basil leaves

3 tablespoons fresh lemon juice, plus more to taste

¼ cup extra-virgin olive oil

A splash of low-sodium vegetable or chicken stock (optional)

With the farro risotto in the pot, season the shrimp and scallops lightly with salt, add them to the risotto, and cook, over medium heat, stirring, until just cooked through, about 3 minutes. Remove the pot from the heat and stir in the tarragon, lemon juice, and oil. Add a little stock or hot water if you'd like the risotto a bit thinner, season with more salt and lemon to taste, and serve right away.

BUYING SCALLOPS: When you're shopping for scallops, the issues of where they're from and how they're harvested aren't typically a big concern—according to Monterey Bay's Seafood Watch, there are way more good options than bad ones. More important is choosing "dry" scallops over "wet" ones. Both terms describe fresh scallops, but "wet" ones are treated with a preservative solution that gives them an off-flavor and unpleasant texture when they're cooked. Scallops aren't always labeled one way or the other, so be sure to ask.

FOUR WAYS WITH WILD RICE

Wild rice—actually the seed of several kinds of marsh grass that grow near the Great Lakes—is a very cool ingredient. It's one of the only grains that's indigenous to North America , and in some areas, one that actually still grows wild and is harvested and processed the old way by Native Americans. Often sold in mixes along with several varieties of rice, the product's distinctive chew, nutty flavor, and incredible aroma deserve your full attention. So these four recipes call for pure wild rice, which you can find in stores or easily order online. And if you can find truly wild wild rice, get that; you'll taste the difference.

SIMPLE WILD RICE

MAKES THREE TIMES AS MUCH COOKED WILD RICE AS DRIED

1. Rinse and drain the wild rice well. Combine equal parts (by volume) wild rice, stock (any kind), and water in a medium heavy pot and bring to a simmer over medium heat. Reduce the heat to low, cover, and cook at a gentle simmer until tender with a slight chew (most of the grains will burst open), 45 minutes to 1 hour. Drain any remaining liquid, transfer the rice to a serving bowl, and serve hot or let cool to room temperature, which is how I like to eat it.

2. Once cooled, the rice keeps in an airtight container in the fridge for up to 5 days.

SPRING

WILD RICE WITH SNAP PEAS, RADISHES, AND FETA

SERVES 4 TO 6
Active time: 20 MINUTES
Start to finish: 20 MINUTES

2 cups snap peas, strings removed (see page 238)
1 small bunch of radishes, greens removed
4 cups cooked wild rice (page 246), still hot in the pot
2 tablespoons extra-virgin olive oil
Big handful of pea shoots or arugula
½ cup crumbled feta cheese
Kosher salt

1. Slice the snap peas thinly on the diagonal. Thinly slice the radishes. Stir the snap peas into the rice pot, and cover. Let the snap peas steam until crisp-tender, about 3 minutes. Drain the rice and peas, transfer to a serving bowl, and let cool to warm or room temperature.

2. Add the radishes, olive oil, pea shoots, feta, and salt to taste. Toss gently but well and serve.

SUMMER

HERBED WILD RICE WITH BALSAMIC AND PINE NUTS

SERVES 4 TO 6
Active time: 20 MINUTES
Start to finish: 20 MINUTES

4 cups cooked wild rice (page 246), cooled to room temperature
Big handful of roughly chopped mixed fresh herbs, such as basil, oregano, cilantro, and dill
2 tablespoons extra-virgin olive oil
2 tablespoons balsamic vinegar
Kosher salt
¼ cup pine nuts, toasted

Put the rice in a large serving bowl. Stir in the herbs, oil, vinegar, and ½ teaspoon salt or more, to taste, then sprinkle on the pine nuts.

FALL

WILD RICE WITH SPINACH, ORANGE ZEST, AND HAZELNUTS

SERVES 4 TO 6
Active time: 20 MINUTES
Start to finish: 20 MINUTES

8 cups packed baby spinach

4 cups cooked wild rice (page 246), still hot, in the pot

2 tablespoons extra-virgin olive oil

1 tablespoon finely grated orange zest

2 tablespoons fresh orange juice

1 tablespoon fresh lemon juice

Kosher salt

⅓ cup hazelnuts, toasted and coarsely chopped

1. Stir the spinach into the rice pot, and cover. Let the spinach steam until wilted, about 3 minutes. Drain the rice and spinach, transfer to a serving bowl, and let cool to warm or room temperature.

2. Stir in the olive oil, orange zest, orange juice, lemon juice, and ½ teapsoon salt or more to taste, then sprinkle on the hazelnuts.

WINTER

WILD RICE WITH QUICK-PICKLED SHALLOTS AND DRIED FRUIT

SERVES 4 TO 6
Active time: 20 MINUTES
Start to finish: 20 MINUTES

1 large shallot, thinly sliced

⅓ cup apple cider vinegar

Kosher salt

4 cups cooked wild rice (page 246), cooled to room temperature

⅓ cup dried cranberries

⅓ cup sliced dried apricots

2 tablespoons extra-virgin olive oil

1. Combine the shallot, vinegar, and ½ teaspoon of salt in a small bowl and mix until the salt dissolves. Let the shallot pickle for at least 10 minutes, preferably an hour.

2. Drain the shallot and stir into the rice along with the cranberries, apricots, oil, and 1 teaspoon salt or more to taste.

FOUR WAYS WITH BULGUR

Bulgur is known almost exclusively as the stuff in the Middle Eastern dish tabbouleh that's not parsley or tomato. That's too bad, because it should be in every pantry in America. Made from grains of whole wheat that have been steamed, dried, and then cracked, bulgur doesn't require cooking so much as rehydration. In other words, it takes barely any effort to make. "Fine" and "medium" bulgur, which take the shortest time to cook, end up a bit like couscous with a slight spring to it. "Coarse" bulgur is great, too—more like rice, but lighter and with that same great springy texture.

SIMPLE BULGUR

MAKES TWICE AS MUCH COOKED BULGUR AS DRIED

1. Put the bulgur in a big heatproof bowl. Put twice the amount of water (by volume) in a saucepan and bring it to a boil over high heat. Stir in a generous pinch of salt and pour the boiling water over the bulgur. Stir well, cover the bowl, and let sit until the bulgur is tender but chewy, about 15 minutes for fine bulgur and 20 to 30 minutes for medium or coarse. Drain any excess liquid and fluff with a fork.

2. Use the bulgur right away or let it cool. It's great hot or cold. Once cooled, it keeps in an airtight container in the fridge for up to 5 days.

SPRING

BULGUR WITH SPINACH, CHICKPEAS, AND PECANS

SERVES 4 TO 6
Active time: 15 MINUTES
Start to finish: 15 MINUTES

2 cups cooked fine or medium bulgur (see page 252)
3 cups baby spinach, washed
One 15-ounce can low-sodium chickpeas or white beans, rinsed and drained
¼ cup extra-virgin olive oil
2 tablespoons apple cider vinegar
Handful of coarsely chopped fresh parsley
Kosher salt
½ cup pecans, toasted and coarsely chopped

In a large serving bowl, fluff the bulgur with a fork, then stir in the spinach, chickpeas, olive oil, vinegar, parsley, and ½ teaspoon salt or more to taste. Sprinkle on the pecans and more salt and vinegar to taste.

SUMMER

BULGUR WITH BLACK-EYED PEAS, TOMATOES, AND LIME

SERVES 4 TO 6
Active time: 15 MINUTES
Start to finish: 15 MINUTES

2 cups cooked fine or medium bulgur (see page 252)
One 14-ounce can black-eyed peas, rinsed and drained
1 pint cherry tomatoes, halved
1 small red onion, finely chopped
Handful of coarsely chopped fresh cilantro
¼ cup extra-virgin olive oil
3 tablespoons fresh lime juice
Kosher salt

In a large serving bowl, fluff the bulgur with a fork, then stir in the black-eyed peas, tomatoes, onion, cilantro, olive oil, lime juice, and ½ teaspoon salt or more to taste.

FALL

BULGUR WITH DELICATA SQUASH AND GREEN OLIVES

SERVES 4 TO 6
Active time: 15 MINUTES
Start to finish: 45 MINUTES

2 medium delicata squash
6 tablespoons extra-virgin olive oil
Kosher salt
2 cups cooked fine or medium bulgur (see page 252)
½ cup sliced green olives
1 teaspoon grated lemon zest
3 to 4 tablespoons fresh lemon juice
Generous pinch of coarsely chopped fresh dill

1. Preheat the oven to 425°F. Cut the ends from the squash so you expose the seeded interior, and get in there with a spoon to scoop out the seeds. Slice it into ¼-inch rounds. Toss the squash on a baking sheet with 2 tablespoons of the oil and 1 teaspoon of salt. Spread it in one layer and roast until the squash is tender and golden browned on the bottoms, 20 to 25 minutes. Let cool.

2. In a large serving bowl, fluff the bulgur with a fork, then stir in the squash, olives, lemon zest, lemon juice, dill, the remaining oil, and ½ teaspoon salt or more to taste.

WINTER

BULGUR WITH POMEGRANATE, ORANGE, AND PISTACHIO

SERVES 4 TO 6
Active time: 10 MINUTES
Start to finish: 10 MINUTES

2 cups cooked fine or medium bulgur (page 252)
¼ cup extra-virgin olive oil
½ cup pomegranate seeds
1 tablespoon finely grated orange zest
Juice from 1 orange
Kosher salt
½ cup chopped pistachios

In a large serving bowl, fluff the bulgur with a fork, then stir in the oil, pomegranate seeds, orange zest, and juice, and ½ teaspoon salt or more to taste. Sprinkle on the pistachios.

NOTE: If you have it, a pinch of saffron added to the hot water you use to soak the bulgur adds great flavor.

FOUR WAYS WITH COUSCOUS

At the White House, couscous frequently saved the day—or at least, the First Family's dinner. Whenever I was running late and rice wasn't an option, I'd turn to the whole-wheat variety of this trusty North African staple, essentially a kind of tiny pasta. The whole-grain version is virtually indistinguishable in flavor and texture from its refined counterpart (something I wish I could say about most Italian pasta), and it offers far more fiber. Plus it's a dream when you're tight on time. Not only does it take just 10 minutes to prepare, you don't even have to monitor the pot. Instead, you stir it into boiling stock or water, turn off the heat, and let it hang out. If I'm in a real rush, I'll just serve it as a side with a drizzle of oil and squeeze of lemon or splash of vinegar. But when I have the time, I like to incorporate vegetables and herbs, so it acts as the centerpiece of a meal.

SIMPLE COUSCOUS

MAKES A LITTLE MORE THAN TWICE AS MUCH COOKED COUSCOUS AS DRIED

1. For every 1¼ cups of couscous, use 1½ cups liquid (I like to use half water and half low-sodium stock for extra flavor). Bring the liquid to a boil over high heat in a pot with a lid. Stir in the couscous, cover the pot, and take it off the heat. Let it sit until the water's been absorbed and the couscous is tender, about 10 minutes. Gently fluff with a fork, breaking up any clumps.

2. Use the couscous right away or let it cool. It's great hot or cold. Once cooled, it keeps in an airtight container in the fridge for up to 5 days.

PRO TIP: Just before serving, try splashing some hot chicken stock on the couscous to keep it moist.

SPRING

COUSCOUS WITH OLIVES, SPINACH, AND SLOW-COOKED GARLIC

SERVES 4 TO 6
Active time: 20 MINUTES
Start to finish: 50 MINUTES

FOR THE GARLIC
1 head of garlic, cloves separated and peeled
1 cup extra-virgin olive oil

FOR THE COUSCOUS
3 cups cooked whole-wheat couscous (page 259), warm
1 cup fresh or thawed frozen shelled edamame
4 cups baby spinach
½ cup very roughly chopped pitted kalamata olives
2 tablespoons red wine vinegar
Kosher salt

1. **MAKE THE GARLIC:** Combine the garlic and oil in a small heavy saucepan and set over very low heat. Let the garlic gently sizzle until smooshably soft and golden in places, about 45 minutes. Store the garlic and oil in the same container in the fridge for up to 2 weeks.

2. **MAKE THE DISH:** Fluff the couscous with a fork and stir in 4 mashed cloves of the cooked garlic and ¼ cup of the reserved garlic oil, edamame, spinach, olives, vinegar, and salt to taste.

SUMMER

COUSCOUS WITH BEETS, ARUGULA, AND PARMESAN

SERVES 4 TO 6
Active time: 15 MINUTES
Start to finish: 1½ HOURS

1 bunch of golden beets (about 4)
3 cups cooked whole-wheat couscous (page 259), warm
6 ounces arugula, coarsely chopped
3 tablespoons fresh lemon juice
¼ cup extra-virgin olive oil
Kosher salt
Big handful of finely grated Parmesan

1. Preheat the oven to 425°F.

2. Trim the stems and greens from the beets, reserving them for another use (they're great sautéed or braised). Wrap the beets tightly in an aluminum foil package, set on a baking sheet, and roast until tender, 1 to 1¼ hours. Let cool until warm, then slip off their skins and cut the beets into bite-sized pieces.

3. Fluff the couscous with a fork and stir in the beets, arugula, lemon juice, the oil, and ½ teaspoon salt or more to taste. Transfer to a serving bowl and scatter the cheese on top.

FALL

COUSCOUS WITH ROASTED CARROTS AND SHALLOTS

SERVES 4 TO 6
Active time: 15 MINUTES
Start to finish: 40 MINUTES

6 to 8 medium carrots, peeled and cut into bite-sized pieces

3 medium shallots, sliced into ¼-inch-thick rounds

¼ cup extra-virgin olive oil

Kosher salt

3 cups cooked whole-wheat couscous (page 259), warm

Handful of coarsely chopped fresh parsley

1 tablespoon apple cider vinegar

1. Preheat the oven to 425°F.

2. Toss the carrots and shallots on a baking sheet with 2 tablespoons of the oil and ½ teaspoon of salt. Spread them out in a single layer and roast until golden brown in spots and tender, 20 to 30 minutes.

3. Fluff the couscous with a fork and stir in the carrots, shallots, parsley, and vinegar along with the remaining 2 tablespoons oil and 1 teaspoon salt. Season with more salt and vinegar to taste. Transfer to a serving bowl.

WINTER

COUSCOUS WITH OLIVES, PIQUILLO PEPPERS, AND PINE NUTS

SERVES 4 TO 6
Active time: 15 MINUTES
Start to finish: 15 MINUTES

3 cups cooked whole-wheat couscous (page 259), warm

One 12-ounce jar roasted piquillo or red bell peppers, drained and sliced

¼ cup sliced pitted green olives

¼ cup pine nuts or almonds, toasted

Handful of coarsely chopped fresh parsley

½ teaspoon dried red pepper flakes

2 tablespoons unsalted butter, melted

Kosher salt

In a large serving bowl, fluff the couscous with a fork and stir in the piquillo peppers, olives, pine nuts, parsley, butter, pepper flakes, and 1 teaspoon salt or more to taste.

FOUR WAYS WITH BEANS

I'm a fan of canned beans. But I like dried beans even more. They'll save you money, and raise the bar on flavor and texture. Because they're so naturally delicious, you don't have to do much to them, except make sure you season them well with salt and maybe add something smoky like bacon or chipotle chiles and some herbs like rosemary and cilantro. When I use canned beans, I like to really dress them up—perhaps with olive oil, herbs, and poached seafood. The good news is you really can't go wrong.

SIMPLE BEANS

There are about as many factions among bean cookers as there are in Congress. Some people hot soak, some cold soak, some add salt only at the last minute, some cook aromatics first thing. I've tried most methods, but always come back to this one, which requires no soaking at all. It works for any dried beans. The keys are buying relatively fresh dried beans (that haven't been on the supermarket shelf for several years) and not turning off the heat until they're creamy. Reserve the flavorful cooking liquid as a vegetarian broth that's great for soups and for moistening simple cooked grains.

MAKES ABOUT 6 CUPS BEANS, PLUS LEFTOVER BEAN BROTH

1 pound dried beans

Several peeled garlic cloves

2 or 3 dried bay leaves

A couple chunks or slices of bacon (optional)

Kosher salt

Water, low-sodium chicken stock, or a combination of both, as needed

1. Pick through the beans and look for stones. It's rare, but you'll occasionally catch something. Give the beans a rinse.

2. Put the beans, garlic, bay leaves, bacon (if using), and a few generous pinches of salt in a large pot. Pour in enough water and/or stock to cover the beans by 2 inches or so. Bring to a boil over high heat, then reduce the heat to low, cover, and cook, adjusting the heat if necessary to maintain a very gentle simmer. Cook until the beans are soft and creamy but before they begin to burst. The timing differs according to your beans and how old they are, but I'd start checking after about 1½ hours. When they're just a touch firmer than you like, season the broth with salt until it tastes great and continue cooking until done.

3. If you're not using them right away, let the beans cool in the cooking liquid and store them and the liquid in an airtight container in the fridge for up to 5 days.

BEAN SALAD
WITH SEAFOOD AND HERBS

SERVES 4 TO 6
Active time: 25 MINUTES
Start to finish: 25 MINUTES

Kosher salt

2 cloves garlic, smashed

½ pound medium shrimp, peeled and halved lengthwise

½ pound cleaned squid (bodies and tentacles), bodies cut into ¼-inch-thick rings

Two 14-ounce cans white beans, rinsed and drained, or 3 cups cooked dried beans (page 264), drained, at room temperature

Big handful of mixed roughly chopped fresh herbs, such as basil, cilantro, dill, parsley, and mint

¼ cup extra-virgin olive oil

1 teaspoon finely grated lemon zest

3 tablespoons fresh lemon juice

1. Bring a medium pot of well-salted water to a boil with the garlic and the remains of the lemon you zested and juiced. Reduce the heat and simmer the shrimp and squid until just cooked through, about 2 minutes. Drain well and let cool.

2. Toss the shrimp and squid in a serving bowl along with the beans, herbs, oil, lemon zest, and lemon juice. Season with salt to taste.

BLACK BEANS
WITH CHIPOTLE AND AVOCADO

SERVES 4 TO 6
Active time: 15 MINUTES
Start to finish: 1¾ HOURS

1 pound dried black beans, picked over for stones (see Note)

3 tablespoons extra-virgin olive oil

2 tablespoons fresh lime juice

1 tablespoon finely chopped canned chipotles in adobo

Kosher salt

2 ripe avocados

Handful of coarsely chopped fresh cilantro

1. Put the beans in a large, heavy pot, cover by 2 inches or so with fresh water, and bring the water to a boil. Cover, reduce the heat to low, and simmer gently until the beans are tender and creamy inside, 1½ to 2 hours, salting it to taste just before the beans are fully tender. Turn off the heat and let the beans sit for 10 minutes. Drain, reserving 1 cup of the bean cooking liquid.

2. In a blender, puree 1 cup of the beans with the reserved 1 cup of liquid (be careful when you blend hot liquid; protect your hand with a kitchen towel or oven mitt and make sure the lid is on tight). Put the rest of the beans in a serving bowl. Stir in the bean puree along with the oil, lime juice, chipotle in adobo, and salt to taste. Cut the avocados into bite-sized pieces, add to the beans along with the cilantro, and serve.

NOTE: To substitute canned beans, use 6 cups, rinsed and drained, and heat in fresh water, just until hot, then drain and proceed from step 2.

YELLOW EYE BEANS

WITH BACON AND ROSEMARY

SERVES 4 TO 6
Active time: 15 MINUTES
Start to finish: 2 HOURS

¼ pound bacon, chopped
2 dried bay leaves
2 fresh thyme sprigs
1 fresh rosemary sprig
1 pound dried yellow eye, cranberry, or white beans, picked over for stones (see Note)
Kosher salt
2 tablespoons apple cider vinegar

1. Put the bacon in a large heavy pot set over medium heat and cook, stirring occasionally, until it releases its fat and turns brown and crisp, 8 to 10 minutes. Stir in the bay leaves, thyme, and rosemary and cook, stirring, for a minute or so.

2. Add the beans along with enough fresh water to cover by 2 inches or so. Raise the heat to bring the water to a boil, then cover and reduce the heat to low and simmer gently until the beans are tender and creamy inside; start checking at about 1½ hours. Just before the beans are tender, season them with 1½ teaspoons of salt, or more to taste. Turn off the heat and let the beans sit for 10 minutes or so. Drain all but 1 cup of the cooking liquid, then stir in the vinegar and more salt to taste.

NOTE: To substitute canned beans, use 6 cups, rinsed and drained. Add them to the bacon-herb mixture with just 1 cup water. Cook until hot, then season as directed.

RED BEANS AND RICE

SERVES 4 TO 6
Active time: 20 MINUTES
Start to finish: 2 HOURS

3 slices bacon, chopped into small pieces
3 garlic cloves, finely chopped
2 dried bay leaves
1 pound dried red beans, picked through for stones (see Note)
Kosher salt
4 cups cooked brown rice (page 230)
4 scallions, thinly sliced

1. Put the bacon in a large heavy pot, set it over medium heat, and cook, stirring occasionally, until it releases its fat, about 5 minutes. Stir in the garlic and bay leaves and cook until the garlic is golden, about 2 minutes.

2. Add the beans along with enough fresh water to cover by 2 inches or so. Raise the heat to bring the water to a boil, then reduce the heat and simmer gently until the beans are tender and creamy inside; start checking at 1½ hours. Just before the beans are tender, season them with salt to taste. Turn off the heat and let the beans sit for 10 minutes or so. Remove and discard the bay leaves and bacon.

3. Stir the red beans with some of their cooking liquid into the brown rice and scallions. Add more liquid as needed, and season to taste with more salt.

NOTE: To substitute canned beans, use 6 cups, rinsed and drained. Add them to the bacon mixture with 1½ cups water, or enough to give them a saucy consistency. Cook until hot, then season.

FOUR WAYS WITH LENTILS

Lentils belong to the same family as beans with one important difference—they take much less time to cook. And in lieu of the creaminess of beans, black and green lentils flaunt a slight bite that I love. It makes them a pleasure, cold in salads or warm in a simple stew. I'm also really into red split lentils, which cook super quickly. These are the lentils I use for making soups, often whizzing them in a blender with stock for a silky texture. And I even get down with sprouted lentils, which you can make yourself from black or green lentils and have a killer crisp snap. Each recipe that follows shows a new side of this versatile legume. Use them to make dinner or as models to inspire your own creations.

SIMPLE LENTILS

MAKES TWICE AS MANY COOKED LENTILS AS DRIED

1. Pick over the lentils for any small stones and rinse. Combine the lentils and enough water to cover by several inches in a large pot. Bring the water to a boil over high heat and add salt so the water tastes slightly salty. Reduce the heat to maintain a gentle simmer and cook, stirring occasionally, until the lentils are tender with a slight bite (but not a crunch). Depending on the lentil, this might take 15 minutes, or it might take 40. Just keep an eye on them and taste frequently. (If you're cooking red or yellow lentils, they will cook down into a thick soup-like consistency; don't drain them.)

2. Drain the lentils in a fine-mesh strainer (or one with small holes so you don't lose any lentils). Use them right away or let cool; they're great hot or cold. Once cooled, they keep in an airtight container in the fridge for up to 5 days.

LENTIL SALAD

WITH ZUCCHINI, TOMATOES, AND HERBS

Sweet summer zucchini and tomatoes are pretty much all you need to make lentils into a satisfying summer salad. But just about any of the summer grain recipes in this chapter would be great with lentils instead, like the sweet roasted beets, peppery arugula, and Parmesan I pair with couscous (page 260) or the eggplant and bell peppers I sauté and toss with quinoa (page 238).

SERVES 4 TO 6
Active time: 15 MINUTES
Start to finish: 15 MINUTES

1 medium zucchini

1 large tomato, cored and chopped

Handful of chopped fresh dill

2 tablespoons extra-virgin olive oil

1 tablespoon white balsamic or white wine vinegar

2 scallions, sliced

2 cups cooked green or black lentils (opposite)

Kosher salt

Grate the zucchini into a large bowl using the large holes on a box grater. Toss with the tomato, dill, olive oil, vinegar, scallions, and lentils. Season with salt to taste and serve.

BRAISED LENTILS
WITH BALSAMIC AND THYME

Green or black are my go-tos when I want lentils to hold their shape—which in this rich, rustic dish makes the difference between braised lentils and lentil mush. The aromatics you use are up to you and should change based on what you like and what you have.

SERVES 4 TO 6
Active time: 15 MINUTES
Start to finish: 50 MINUTES

2 tablespoons extra-virgin olive oil
1 large onion, cut into ½-inch pieces
1 large carrot, cut into ½-inch pieces
1 celery stalk, cut into ½-inch pieces
2 dried bay leaves
5 cups low-sodium chicken stock
2 cups green or black lentils, picked over for stones
Handful of coarsely chopped fresh parsley
1 teaspoon coarsely chopped fresh thyme leaves
4 to 5 tablespoons balsamic vinegar
Kosher salt

Heat the oil in a medium heavy pot over medium heat until it shimmers. Stir in the onion, carrot, celery, and bay leaves and cook, stirring occasionally, until the vegetables are golden in spots, about 6 minutes. Add the stock and lentils, bring to a simmer, and simmer until the lentils are tender but not falling apart, 30 to 40 minutes. Stir in the parsley, thyme, ¼ cup of the balsamic, and 1 teaspoon salt. Season with more balsamic and salt to taste.

MONA'S LENTIL SOUP

Mona is part of the village of people who raised me, a family friend who immigrated from Egypt. For her, feeding the people she loves is pure pleasure—unless you happen to insult her by having any less than three servings of her lentil soup. Lucky for all of us, it was so damn good.

SERVES 4 TO 6
Active time: 15 MINUTES
Start to finish: 1 HOUR

2 tablespoons extra-virgin olive oil

1 large onion, cut into ½-inch pieces

3 medium carrots, cut into ½-inch pieces

4 garlic cloves, thinly sliced

1½ teaspoons ground cumin

1 pound orange, red, or yellow split lentils

6 cups low-sodium vegetable stock or water

Kosher salt

Lemon wedges

Toasted pita, for serving

1. Heat the oil in a medium heavy pot over medium heat until it shimmers. Stir in the onion, carrots, and garlic and cook, stirring occasionally, until the onion is translucent, 5 minutes or so. Stir in the cumin and toast it, stirring until very fragrant, about 1 minute.

2. Add the lentils, stir for a minute or so, then add the stock. Let it come to simmer and cook until the lentils fall apart, about 45 minutes. Stir in 2 teaspoons salt or more to taste.

3. Blend in a blender until smooth, securing the lid and protecting your hand with a towel. Season with more salt to taste and serve with the lemon wedges and pita.

SPROUTED LENTILS
WITH RADISHES, CHIVES, AND LEMON

Sprouting lentils yourself is a culinary science project with tasty results. When you soak lentils, then leave them covered for a few days with a damp paper towel, you jump-start the germination process. By the time you see a little sprout popping out of each one, the dried lentil has developed an enticing crunch, no cooking needed, like peas straight out of the pod. And bonus, the already great-for-you legume gets a little nutritional boost.

That said, if the lentils are too old, they won't sprout, so for this recipe, dusty bags from the supermarket aren't ideal. Try to buy lentils from a place where there's plenty of turnover. If they don't sprout, no worries: Just cook them like you would regular lentils.

Of course, this particular combination of ingredients can be taken in many different directions. Radishes are crunchy and sweet, as are cucumbers, red onions, and bell peppers. Chives taste green and fresh, but so do parsley, tarragon, cilantro, and dill. Lemon provides brightness, but so could red wine vinegar or lime juice.

SERVES 4 TO 6
Active time: 10 MINUTES
Start to finish: 5 DAYS (INCLUDES SPROUTING TIME)

1 cup green or black lentils, picked over for stones

6 small radishes, thinly sliced

Handful of thinly sliced fresh chives

3 tablespoons extra-virgin olive oil

2 tablespoons fresh lemon juice

Kosher salt

1. Rinse the lentils under cold water and put them in a bowl with enough fresh cold water to cover by 2 inches or so. Let the lentils soak at room temperature overnight, then drain them well in a colander. Transfer the lentils to large bowl and cover them with a damp paper towel. Leave them at room temperature to sprout tails, ½ to 1 inch long, gently stirring them once a day and keeping the paper towel damp. This should take 3 to 4 days.

2. Rinse the lentils, drain them very well, and toss them in a serving bowl with the radishes, chives, olive oil, lemon juice, and 1 teaspoon salt or more to taste.

Acknowledgments

Thank you to JJ Goode for your help in writing this book. Your patience, good humor, and talent have made this book what it is and I am forever grateful. To Francis Lam—editor of editors—for all you did to make this book better. To Doris Cooper, Aaron Wehner, Danielle Daitch, Jen Wang, Stephanie Huntwork, Ada Yonenaka, Kim Tyner, Kate Tyler, Erica Gelbard, and the rest of the team at Clarkson Potter, for there would be no book without your support. To Aubrie Pick, Bessma Khalaf, Molly Shuster, Joy Howard, Erika Iroff, Alistair Turnbull, and John Lingenfelter, the crew who photographed this book, for bringing my food to life. And to Ian Knauer for making sure these recipes work!

To all the farmers, winemakers, home cooks, gardeners, school chefs, kids, and everyone who gave me little gifts of flavor or insight along the way. Special thanks to the chefs that let me into their kitchens and to the cooks who taught me so much. To Dean Zanella, who gave me my first gig at 312 Chicago. To Paul Kahan and Koren Grieveson, who deeply shaped my approach to food. And most of all, to Christian Domschitz and Alois Traint, the chefs who let this yankee into their world and set a high bar that has guided everything I have done since, both inside and outside the kitchen.

To chef Cris Comerford, Tommy Kurpradit, Tafari Campbell, and Adam Collick for the years of making history and good times in the White House Kitchen. To Vaughn, Buddy, and all of the butlers for the endless jokes that made the job all the more fun. To Dale Hainey, Jim Adams, and the rest of the Park Service crew who help keep the garden alive and beautiful. And to everyone in the Obama administration who helped us accomplish more on food, health, and sustainability than any administration in the history of our nation. This book is an ode to what we accomplished together.

To President Barack Obama and First Lady Michelle Obama. What can I say? Thank you for the years of friendship, for the early-morning workouts, for the mentorship, and for giving me a shot to make a difference outside of the kitchen. I hope I didn't disappoint.

How do you truly thank your parents and sister? You apologize! Sorry for all the stress I caused. Thank you for a lifetime of keeping me on track.

And to Alex, my brilliant, gorgeous, hilarious wife and mother of my perfect child. Not sure how I got so lucky. You make me a better man. I love you.

Index

Y

Z

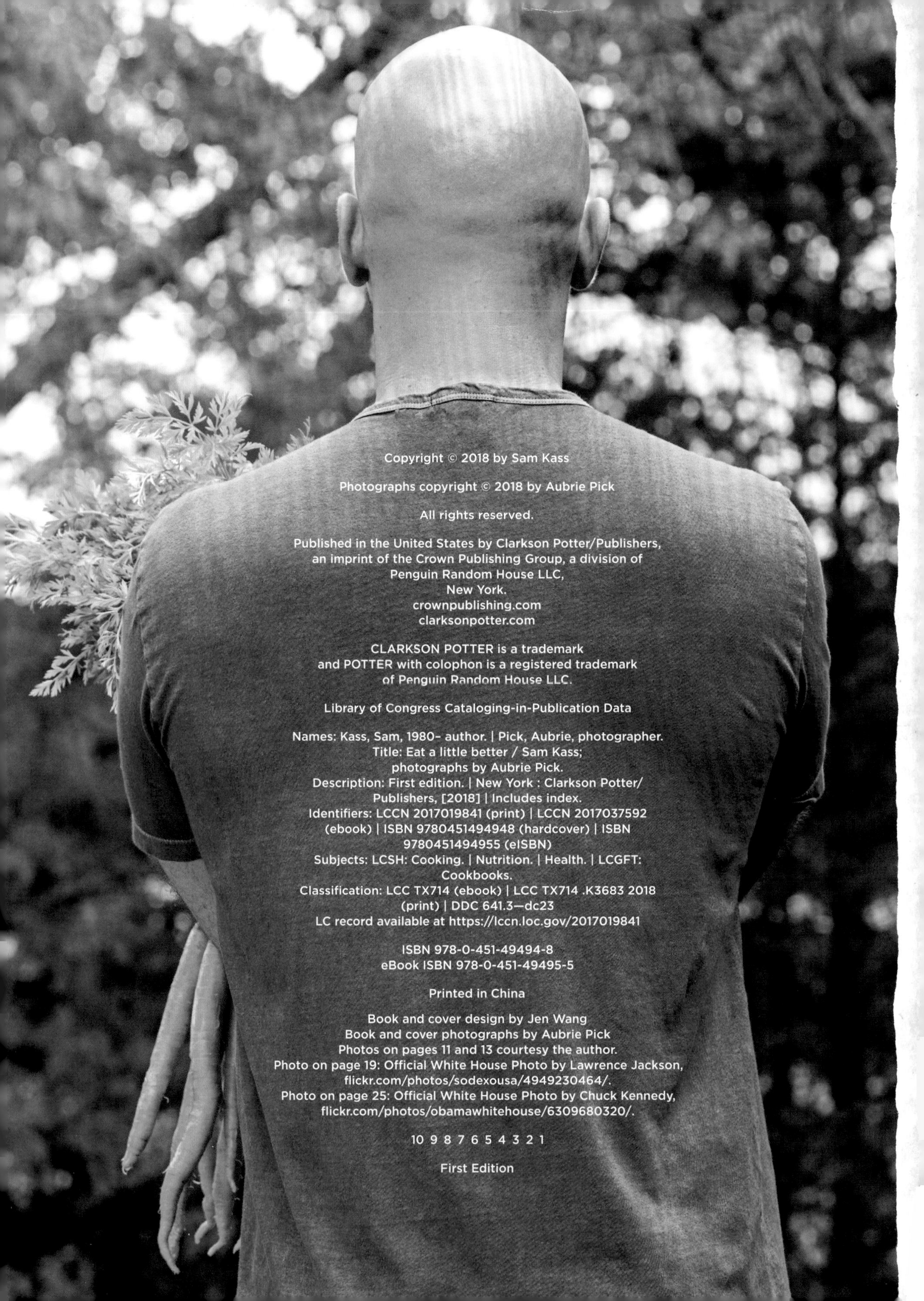

Published in the United States by Clarkson Potter/Publishers,
an imprint of the Crown Publishing Group, a division of
Penguin Random House LLC,
New York.
crownpublishing.com
clarksonpotter.com

CLARKSON POTTER is a trademark
and POTTER with colophon is a registered trademark
of Penguin Random House LLC.

Library of Congress Cataloging-in-Publication Data

Names: Kass, Sam, 1980– author. | Pick, Aubrie, photographer.
Title: Eat a little better / Sam Kass;
photographs by Aubrie Pick.
Description: First edition. | New York : Clarkson Potter/
Publishers, [2018] | Includes index.
Identifiers: LCCN 2017019841 (print) | LCCN 2017037592
(ebook) | ISBN 9780451494948 (hardcover) | ISBN
9780451494955 (eISBN)
Subjects: LCSH: Cooking. | Nutrition. | Health. | LCGFT:
Cookbooks.
Classification: LCC TX714 (ebook) | LCC TX714 .K3683 2018
(print) | DDC 641.3—dc23
LC record available at https://lccn.loc.gov/2017019841

ISBN 978-0-451-49494-8
eBook ISBN 978-0-451-49495-5

Printed in China

Book and cover design by Jen Wang
Book and cover photographs by Aubrie Pick
Photos on pages 11 and 13 courtesy the author.
Photo on page 19: Official White House Photo by Lawrence Jackson,
flickr.com/photos/sodexousa/4949230464/.
Photo on page 25: Official White House Photo by Chuck Kennedy,
flickr.com/photos/obamawhitehouse/6309680320/.

10 9 8 7 6 5 4 3 2 1

First Edition